"As I began reading   ed
of Martin Luther's comment that   isy
is a meadow.' Many believers will have read through John 13–17
more than once and may even feel they have a pretty good grasp
of its meaning. I was one of them—until I read Sinclair Ferguson's
Lessons from the Upper Room! As he wisely says, 'Our minds are
far too finite to understand fully what the infinite Lord of all is
doing,' but the more I read, the more I felt drawn into that amazing upper room, listening, learning—and loving what the Savior
was saying. Crystal-clear illustrations and warm-hearted applications permeate these pages—and I will never forget the author's
allegory that he calls 'The Stranger in Smokeland'! *Lessons from
the Upper Room* is Ferguson at his finest. Get two copies—and
share the treasure with someone else!"

—Dr. John Blanchard
Preacher, teacher, apologist, and author
Banstead, England

"Few passages in Scripture are as influential as John's Farewell Discourse, but its message is often elusive. Sinclair Ferguson helps
us put the pieces of the puzzle in place in the light of the whole
Bible. Pull up a chair and listen as Ferguson helps us understand
what we overhear from Jesus' speaking to His disciples and praying to His Father. This book unpacks the drama and meaning of
the last night of Jesus' life and richly explains how this is good
news for us today. This is vintage Ferguson—a sensitive reading
of the biblical text in light of the whole Bible, with consummate
focus on our Savior and His work. Whether you're familiar with

this passage or have never read it before, this book is sure to be encouraging, edifying, and enlightening. Pick up this book—you'll be glad you did!"

—Dr. Brandon D. Crowe
Professor of New Testament,
Westminster Theological Seminary
Philadelphia

"Sinclair Ferguson is one of the few writers in this or any generation of whom it can be said that anything he writes is a must-read. In this book, he transports us to the upper room with Jesus to witness the last hours of His earthly ministry. You will feel like you are there, sitting next to the Lord, savoring the meal, hearing the anxious inquires of the disciples, listening to words that will change everything. Whether you have walked with Christ for many years or have just become a Christian, Dr. Ferguson's years of meditation on these chapters, combined with his unequaled pastoral wisdom, make these pages uniquely accessible to a variety of readers. It is the finest nontechnical treatment of John 13–17 in print."

—Dr. Gabriel N.E. Fluhrer
Associate minister of discipleship,
First Presbyterian Church
Columbia, S.C.

Lessons from the Upper Room

Lessons from the Upper Room

Upper

The Heart
of the Savior

Room

SINCLAIR B. FERGUSON

 LIGONIER MINISTRIES

Lessons from the Upper Room: The Heart of the Savior
© 2021 by Sinclair B. Ferguson

Published by Ligonier Ministries
421 Ligonier Court, Sanford, FL 32771
Ligonier.org

Printed in Ann Arbor, Michigan
Cushing-Malloy, Inc.
0000122
First edition, third printing

ISBN 978-1-64289-319-9 (Paperback)
ISBN 978-1-64289-320-5 (ePub)
ISBN 978-1-64289-321-2 (Kindle)

Cover design: Ligonier Creative
Tintoretto, *Two Apostles*, late 16th century. Image courtesy of The Barnes Foundation.
Interior design and typeset: Katherine Lloyd, The DESK

Scripture quotations are from the ESV® Bible (The Holy Bible, English Standard Version®), copyright © 2001 by Crossway, a publishing ministry of Good News Publishers. Used by permission. All rights reserved.

Library of Congress Control Number: 2020952348

Now before the Feast of the Passover,
when Jesus knew that his hour had come
to depart out of this world to the Father,
having loved his own who were in the world,
he loved them to the end.

—JOHN 13:1

To

My Dorothy
and
Ruth

Loving Helpers
Wise Counselors
Devoted Homemakers
Best Friends

With Love and Gratitude

Contents

Introduction 1

1. The Mind of Christ 3

2. Understanding and Blessing. 21

3. From Trouble to Glory 35

4. Atmospheric Changes. 45

5. *Via, Veritas, Vita* 61

6. Threefold Spirit. 85

7. The True Vine 105

8. Hated but Helped. 119

9. Why? Why? Why?. 141

10. Confusion before Clarity 157

11. The Heart of Christ Opened .177

12. The Father's Gift. 197

13. He Prays for Me 211

Notes. 225

Index. 233

About the Author. 241

Introduction

Lessons from the Upper Room is an invitation to spend a few hours with Jesus' disciples, listening to His teaching and overhearing Him pray—both for them and for you. It is based on John's gospel, chapters 13 through 17. Here, in five chapters, in only 155 verses, and in less than four thousand words we are given what the Puritan writer Thomas Goodwin called "a window into Christ's heart."[1]

This section of John's gospel has meant a great deal to me since my student days, and I have often thought of writing a book on it simply for my own benefit. But the immediate stimulus behind *Lessons from the Upper Room* came from recording a series of twelve short messages on these chapters for Ligonier Ministries in 2014.

In a sense, these pages are "the book of the movie." As is often the case, the two are not identical. In this instance, the book has been written several years after the recordings were made and it is probably more than 50 percent longer than a transcript of the original messages. Anyone present at the recording sessions, or who has watched them, will find echoes of them in these pages. But the book is a fuller exposition of these wonderful chapters, and so I hope that even those present at the recording, or who have watched or listened to them, will find it rewarding.

Even so, *Lessons from the Upper Room* is by no means a complete exposition of John 13–17. If that were attempted—to adapt some words of John himself—an entire bookcase could not contain the books that would be written!

Nor are these pages a commentary in any technical sense. They are, perhaps, more like the "audio description" function on my "smart" TV set. This facility provides a running commentary on the action taking place on the screen to help those who can follow the dialogue but are too visually handicapped to see it. So I hope that there will be moments in reading these pages when readers will feel—as I have in writing them—that they are "there" in the upper room itself, meeting with Christ, watching Him, and listening to Him teach and pray.

It is always a privilege to serve alongside Ligonier Ministries and its publishing arm, and I am indebted especially to the audio-video production team and to the editorial team, who, over the years, have become not only guides but friends. I am also grateful to those who joined me for two intensive days of filming during which we worked our way together through Jesus' Farewell Discourse. And as with everything else in life, my chief debt under God is to my wife, Dorothy, and to the family we love.

1

The Mind of Christ

John 13:1–12

Now before the Feast of the Passover, when Jesus knew that his hour had come to depart out of this world to the Father, having loved his own who were in the world, he loved them to the end. During supper, when the devil had already put it into the heart of Judas Iscariot, Simon's son, to betray him, Jesus, knowing that the Father had given all things into his hands, and that he had come from God and was going back to God, rose from supper. He laid aside his outer garments, and taking a towel, tied it around his waist. Then he poured water into a basin and began to wash the disciples' feet and to wipe them with the towel that was wrapped around him. He came to Simon Peter, who said to him, "Lord, do you wash my feet?" Jesus answered him, "What I am doing you do not understand now, but afterward you will understand." Peter said to him, "You shall never wash my feet." Jesus answered him, "If I do not wash you, you have no share with me." Simon Peter said to him, "Lord, not my feet only but also my hands and my head!" Jesus said to him, "The one who has bathed does not need to wash, except for his feet, but is completely clean. And you are clean, but not every one of you." For he knew who was to betray him; that was why he said, "Not all of you are clean."

When he had washed their feet and put on his outer garments and resumed his place, he said to them, "Do you understand what I have done to you?"

In our imagination, let us climb the stairs leading to an upper room on a house in Jerusalem. Here we can eavesdrop on what transpired during the late afternoon and evening of the day before the crucifixion of Jesus of Nazareth.

Thirteen men have come together for a Passover meal. One will leave early on a mission of betrayal. The remaining twelve will later make their way to the garden of Gethsemane.

From there they will be scattered. One will be taken by force on a nightmare journey.

It will bring Him first to the deposed high priest Annas. From there He will be taken to the house of Annas' son-in-law Caiaphas, now the high priest. He will then be taken to the Judgment Hall of Pontius Pilate the Roman governor, then to King Herod and back to Pilate before finally being led along the Via Dolorosa to the cross of Calvary. There He will be crucified.

By this time tomorrow, Friday, the lifeless body of Jesus of Nazareth will be carried to a garden tomb.

But this is not the end, just the end of the beginning. For early on Sunday morning, He will rise again from the dead. He now lives forever as a Prince and Savior. All this is still to come. For now, we have arrived at the upper room.

In less than twenty-four hours, the Savior will be dead—crucified. Well aware that this is His certain destiny, He wants to show His disciples that He loves them to the end.

Soon He will dismiss one of them—Judas Iscariot—from the room to betray Him. Shortly afterward, He will tell another of them—Simon Peter—that before a new day dawns, he will have denied Him three times. Before they leave, He will pray the longest prayer recorded in the New Testament. It is truly "the Lord's Prayer." In it, He will disclose the intimacy of His relationship to His heavenly Father and His disciples will overhear expressions of His love and care for them, but also for all those who—like ourselves—will become His disciples in the future.

These are dramatic moments.

But first, let us listen to John's account of how the evening began:

Now before the Feast of the Passover, when Jesus knew that his hour had come to depart out of this world to the Father, having loved his own who were in the world, he loved them to the end. During supper, when the devil had already put it into the heart of Judas Iscariot, Simon's son, to betray him, Jesus, knowing that the Father had given all things into his hands, and that he had come from God and was going back to God, rose from supper. He laid aside his outer garments, and taking a towel, tied it around his waist. Then he poured water into a basin and began to wash the disciples' feet and to wipe them with the towel that was wrapped around him. He came to Simon Peter, who said to him, "Lord, do you wash my feet?" Jesus answered him, "What I am doing you do not understand now, but afterward you will understand." Peter said to him, "You shall never wash my feet." Jesus answered him, "If I do not wash you, you have no share with me." Simon Peter said to him, "Lord, not my feet only but also my hands and my head!" Jesus said to him, "The one who has bathed does not need to wash, except for his feet, but is completely clean. And you are clean, but not every one of you." For he knew who was to betray him; that was why he said, "Not all of you are clean."

And then,

When he had washed their feet and put on his outer garments [He] resumed his place . . .

Every time we read a passage from the Bible, two different contexts meet together. That is certainly true here.

Contexts

We inevitably read these verses from within our own context.

Because "the sacred writings . . . are able to make you wise for salvation through faith in Christ Jesus" (2 Tim. 3:15), these verses will naturally cause us to think about personal questions like, "Is the Lord Jesus Christ central in my thinking and living?" An honest answer would probably be, "Yes, but not always, and never as much as He deserves to be." As Christians, we are no longer what we once were by nature, but we know we have not yet become what Christ has called us to be. We want to know, trust, and love Him better.

These chapters help us do that by moving Him to the center of our vision and showing us His grace.

But we also need to learn to read these chapters within their own context.

John's gospel has a clear and relatively simple shape.

It begins with a prologue (1:1–18)—a passage we often read at Christmastime.

It ends with an epilogue (21:1–25)—the passage in which Jesus restores Simon Peter to his Apostolic ministry.

In between, the gospel is divided into two parts or books.

Part 1 (1:19–12:50) is sometimes called the Book of Signs. The words and works of Jesus together point to His identity as the Messiah and Savior. So, for example, He claims to be "the Light of the World." Those who follow Him will not walk in darkness (8:12). He then illustrates this by giving sight to a man who was born blind (ch. 9).

There are seven signs recorded in chapters 1 to 12.[1] But then the Book of Signs ends abruptly: "When Jesus had said these things, he departed and hid himself from them. Though he had done so many signs before them, they still did not believe in him, so that the word spoken by the prophet Isaiah might be fulfilled: 'Lord, who has believed what he heard from us, and to whom has the arm of the Lord been revealed?'" (John 12:36b–38, quoting Isa. 53:1).

Part 2 (13:1–20:31) is the Book of the Passion or, as it is sometimes called, the Book of Glory. As it opens, we have been transported, without explanation, to a room above a house in Jerusalem. It is Thursday afternoon of Passover Week, and a meal is already underway. As far as we know, only thirteen men are in the room—Jesus and His chosen Apostles. Now the glory that Jesus has hidden from a world that has rejected Him will increasingly be revealed to the disciples who trusted and loved Him.

John's "Inside Story"

John's gospel has a quite different feel from the first three Gospels. That is well expressed in a comment made by John Calvin:

> The other three are more copious in their narrative of the life and death of Christ, but *John dwells more largely on the doctrine by which the office of Christ, together with the power of his death and resurrection, is unfolded.* . . .
>
> All of them had the same object in view, to point out Christ, *the three former exhibit his body, if we may be permitted to use the expression, but John exhibits his soul.* On this account, I am accustomed to say that this Gospel is a key to open the door for understanding the rest; for whoever shall understand the power of Christ, as it is here strikingly portrayed, will afterwards read with advantage what the others relate about the Redeemer who was manifested.[2]

The Synoptic Gospels (Matthew, Mark, and Luke) show us "His body"—they tell the story from the outside, as it were. But the nearer John's gospel gets to its climax the more we learn about what was "going on inside" our Lord.

This is preeminently true in chapters 13 through 17. Here we are invited to listen in as Jesus patiently instructs His closest friends as they sit around Him during a Passover meal. It would have lasted several hours—truly memorable hours with the Master!

The narrative begins with Jesus showing His disciples that "he loved them to the end" (John 13:1)—and what true love is really like. Characteristically, He gives a sign—He washes the disciples' feet. Then He provides an explanation and asks: "Do you understand the meaning of this sign? Do you see what it means for Me? And do you understand the implications it has for you?"

Doubtless the room had fallen silent.

This was a very private gathering—only Jesus and the Twelve. No house-servant had welcomed them; no one had washed the street grime from their sandaled feet.

And clearly, they had all been too proud to do it—either for Jesus or for one another. In fact, Luke tells us that the disciples had been arguing with each other about which of them was "the greatest" (Luke 22:24–27). In sharp contrast, Jesus told them, "I am among you as the one who serves." Perhaps it was at this point that He rose from table.

In this world, disciples did not wash each other's feet—that was a servant's work. But now the Master is doing it!

When Jesus kneels down before Simon Peter, however, it is too much for him. Appalled and resistant, he breaks the silence: "Lord, do you wash my feet?"

Jesus answers: "If I do not wash you, you have no share with me" (John 13:8).

Clearly something deeper is going on here than Jesus merely removing dust and dirt. This is a prophetic action—like those performed by Jeremiah and Ezekiel.[3] He is acting out a parable of the gospel, showing them by means of a dramatic sign both who He is and what He has come to do. Here, in the foot-washing, He reveals both His person and His work, both His identity and the purpose of His ministry.

One of the best ways to understand the inner significance of these verses is to look at them side by side with the Apostle Paul's teaching about the Lord Jesus in Philippians 2:6–9:

John 13:3–5, 12	Philippians 2:6–9
Jesus . . . knowing . . . he had come from God	Though he was in the form of God
rose from supper	[He] did not count equality with God a thing to be grasped
laid aside his outer garments	but emptied himself
and taking a towel	taking the form of a servant
poured water into a basin	he humbled himself
and began to wash the disciples' feet	becoming obedient to the point of death, even death on a cross
he . . . put on his outer garments and resumed his place	God has highly exalted him and bestowed on him the name that is above every name

Point by point, Jesus is acting out symbolically what Paul describes theologically—how He came from the highest glory of heaven, into the depths of our human condition, took the form of a slave, and accomplished our cleansing from sin by His death on the cross, and then was exalted to the right hand of the Father.

John invites us to follow what our Lord does in five stages.

Origin

Just as Paul tells us about what was going on in the mind of Christ, John tells us that Jesus is conscious of His divine origin and His mission:

Now before the Feast of the Passover, when Jesus knew his hour had come to depart out of this world to the Father, having loved his own who were in the world, he loved them to the end. . . . When the devil had put it into the heart of Judas Iscariot, Simon's son, to betray him . . . (John 13:1, 2)

He knew that he was going to be betrayed, but He knew something else . . .

Jesus, knowing that the Father had given all things into his hands, and that he had come from God and was going to God, rose from supper . . . (v. 3)

Watch Him:
He rises from his position as host at the table
He begins to disrobe
He wraps a servant's towel round his waist
He fills a basin with water
He now washes his disciples' dirty feet

In a sense, this is just as clearly a "prologue" to Book 2 of John's gospel as John 1:1–18 was to Book 1. In this opening scene, Jesus is "acting out" what the prologue had described in elevated terms:

> In the beginning was the Word, and the Word was with God (*pros ton theon*), and the Word was God.

But the Word who was with God came down to be with us:

> The Word became flesh and dwelt among us . . .

Notice then the first stage: Jesus is conscious of His divine origin. He knows that the Father has given everything into His hands. He knows that He is coequal with the Father in dignity, majesty, glory, and power. He knows that He is now "going back to God [*pros ton theon*]." Here John, significantly surely, uses exactly the same phrase with which he had introduced Jesus in John 1:1. He was *pros ton theon*. He had been from all eternity "toward" or "face-to-face with" God.

But then comes the second stage—His profound humiliation. He had come to be "face-to-face with" man.

Humiliation

Linger for a moment on John's commentary: "Jesus, knowing that the Father had given all things into his hands . . ."

If you were going to finish that sentence, surely you would write, "Jesus . . . then displayed the majesty of the One who possesses all authority in the universe."

But no. What happens is that in the full knowledge that He is Lord of all, the Son of God humbles Himself. He takes off His outer clothing. He goes to the corner of the room where a large jar of water and a small basin stand. He now wraps the servant's towel around Himself.

The only sound to break the silence is water being poured into the basin. Now Jesus begins to wash the feet of disciples who have been too self-invested to wash each other's feet.

Here, in dramatic form, the Son of God, the Word made flesh, gives us a picture of the wonder of His incarnation and His humility.

Thinking about this scene may help us understand Paul's comment: He "emptied himself" (Phil. 2:7).

Scholars have long discussed and debated the meaning of these words.

Did the Son of God empty Himself of all the attributes of His divinity? Or as Charles Wesley has taught centuries of Christians to sing, is it more accurate to say that He "emptied himself of all but love"?[4] Did He somehow cease to be the eternal God for His life span, but then resume that role? Or what?

God's Son "emptied" Himself not by subtraction from His deity but by addition, by His assumption of our frail humanity. He did not cease to be truly divine when He became truly human. He did not empty out from His deity anything intrinsic to that deity. But He devoted Himself to saving us by assuming our nature. The One who never ceased to be "in the form of God" took "the form of a servant" with the accompanying life of deep humiliation. He gave all that He ever was to us and for us when He took our human nature. And He did so in order to take away our sin. He "emptied himself" not by evacuating Himself of the eternal attributes He possessed but by taking temporal attributes He did not possess.

Not for a moment did the Son of God abdicate His lordship over "all things" (John 13:3). In fact, the marvel of the humility and grace He displays here depends on the fact that it is as undiminished deity that He washes dirty feet. Had He emptied Himself of His deity, the foot-washing would have been a truly humble act. But it would simply have been the humble service of a man to his equals or of a good man to others less fortunate than himself. But this is the humble service of God to man—and not just to man but to sinful man.

This points to a third element in Jesus' ministry.

Salvation

Go back for a moment to Simon Peter's protest.

Apparently, all Peter sees here are his own dirty feet and Jesus gazing into his eyes as He is about to wash them. So, he instinctively protests.

We would all do that, surely.

But Jesus says, "Peter, you're not getting the point here. If I don't do this—if you refuse the sign of what I have come to do, you are rejecting the reality to which it points, My dying on the cross to wash away your sins—then you will have no share in the salvation that I have come to bring."

Peter goes from one extreme to the other, from "you will never wash my feet" to "wash my hands and my head too!" He still cannot see clearly. The foot-washing is a picture of what Jesus does for our cleansing and justification. Since Peter has already been made "clean"—he had, after all, trusted Christ and confessed his faith in Him—what he needs is the cleansing power of Christ to continue to work in his life. As the Westminster divines pointed out, we are sanctified through the same union with Christ into which we are regenerated.[5]

Peter is clean but still needs to be cleansed. But, Jesus adds, "Not all of you are clean." By recording these words, John is highlighting the fact that there is a dark background to this scene and another dimension to Christ's saving work. Satan is present in the shadows: "The devil had already put it into the heart of Judas Iscariot . . . to betray him" (John 13:2).

Satan had long been at work. This is the backstory to all four Gospels. The enemy—who first of all sought to prevent Jesus from going to the cross by destroying His life in Herod's pogrom of the Bethlehem infants—had pursued Him from His baptism at the River Jordan onward (Luke 4:1, 13). And now he has invaded the disciple band itself. In a few minutes, he will have "entered into" its treasurer, Judas Iscariot (John 13:27).

Once before he had invaded the camp of Jesus' closest disciples, using Simon Peter to try to divert Him from the road to Calvary (Matt. 16:21–23). He had failed. Did that failure lead to a change in his tactics? For now, he seems to be trying to disrupt the divine plan of salvation by forcing Jesus to His death according to the satanic timetable rather than the Father's one.

But Jesus is Lord. He is still master of the situation and takes each step according to His Father's plan.

John makes this clear: Jesus sovereignly dismisses Judas from the room. "What you are going to do, do quickly," He tells him (John 13:27). This will not be the last indication John gives us that "all things" are in our Lord's hands.

There is a sharp contrast here, then, between the purposes of God and the activity of Satan: Jesus knew that Satan had put it into the heart of Judas Iscariot to betray Him (v. 2), but He also knew that the Father had put everything into His hands (v. 3). Against that backcloth, then, He rose from supper and washed the feet of His beloved disciples.

The grand narrative behind these verses can be traced back to its origin in Genesis 3:15. From page 3 onward, the Bible is the record of how the Seed of the woman and the seed of the serpent are in perpetual conflict until the day dawns when the serpent himself will crush the heel of the Seed of the woman but in the process will be dealt a crushing death blow.

What we are witnessing here is the beginning of the climax of this promise. Satan has come to indwell Judas Iscariot in order to crush Jesus. But by contrast with Satan and Judas, Jesus is obedient to the will of the Father.

John brings out the contrast in telling fashion. He writes that Satan had "thrown it" into the heart of Judas Iscariot to betray Jesus (John 13:2). By contrast, Jesus "threw water into a basin" (v. 5). The same verb (Greek *ballō*) is used in both statements. Although His heel will be crushed, our Lord will fatally crush the serpent "by becoming obedient to the point of death, even death on a cross" (Phil. 2:8).

Now a fourth stage in Christ's work is portrayed.

Exaltation

Jesus has knelt before each of the Twelve and washed their feet—those of Simon Peter but also of Judas Iscariot. He puts on His clothes again "and resumed his place" (John 13:12). "Do you understand what this is all about?" He asks.

The verb John uses here, "put on" (Greek *lambanō*), echoes its earlier use in Jesus' words about His resurrection: "I lay down my life that I may take it up again. No one takes it from me, but I lay it down of my own accord. I have authority to lay it down, and I have authority to take it up" (John 10:17–18).

What a vivid picture Jesus is painting for His disciples. He is going to be humiliated and crucified. But He is laying down His life voluntarily, and He will take it up again sovereignly and return to His place of eternal honor. Sometimes the painting of a great artist will reflect the work of an earlier master from whom he has learned. In a similar way, John's picture here reflects Old Testament prophecies—and none more clearly than Isaiah's description of the Suffering Servant (Isa. 52:13–53:12).

In the Scottish state elementary school I attended, religious education was a compulsory subject. Looking back now, I suspect that the teacher I had when I was about eight took the easy way out: she made us learn by heart the words of Isaiah 53:1–12. No one told me then—and I suspect my teacher did not know—that this passage really begins in Isaiah 52:13. There the Servant who suffers so grievously is introduced as someone who will be exalted because of His suffering, and as a result will "sprinkle many nations."

The prophetic picture painted by Isaiah is now symbolically dramatized here by Jesus. He gets up, He kneels down, He washes, but then He resumes His place. Before they have left the room, His disciples will overhear Him speaking to His Father about His future exaltation. Because of His humiliation, culminating in His death and burial, God will highly exalt Him and give Him the name that is above every name. One day, at the name of Jesus, every knee will bow—in heaven, on earth, and even under the earth—and every tongue confess that He is Lord (Phil. 2:9–11).

Here, then, Jesus kneels. But now He rises, takes His garments again, and resumes His place. Now the room listens to Him. And so it will be when the Father exalts Him: all authority will be His and all nations will hear of Him, and all creation will eventually bow before Him. He will be crowned Lord of all (Matt. 28:18–20; 1 Cor. 15:20–28).

This brings us to a fifth detail painted into this portrait of the grace of our Lord Jesus Christ.

Implication

"Do you understand what I have done to you?" Jesus asks (John 13:12). In other words, "Do you see the significance of this—for Me—and for you too?"

"I have washed your feet," He says. "If you understand what I have done, it will lead to a transformation in you; you will begin to do what you failed to do before we sat down to eat; you will follow My example. You will kneel down before your fellow disciples, and by your humble service say to them, 'I am your servant, for Jesus' sake'" (cf. 2 Cor. 4:5).

There is a glimpse here of the glory of our Savior—who He is, what He has done for us, how He has been exalted, and where He is now.

In addition, there is a challenging application.

Knowing is one thing, Jesus says, but doing is another.

Has knowing all this made any difference in my life? Am I a servant of others?

Only those who do as well as hear are blessed (John 13:17). But thinking about that must wait for the next chapter.

2
—

Understanding and Blessing

John 13:12–20

When he had washed their feet and put on his outer garments and resumed his place, he said to them, "Do you understand what I have done to you? You call me Teacher and Lord, and you are right, for so I am. If I then, your Lord and Teacher, have washed your feet, you also ought to wash one another's feet. For I have given you an example, that you also should do just as I have done to you. Truly, truly, I say to you, a servant is not greater than his master, nor is a messenger greater than the one who sent him. If you know these things, blessed are you if you do them. I am not speaking of all of you; I know whom I have chosen. But the Scripture will be fulfilled, 'He who ate my bread has lifted his heel against me.' I am telling you this now, before it takes place, that when it does take place you may believe that I am he. Truly, truly, I say to you, whoever receives the one I send receives me, and whoever receives me receives the one who sent me."

The fourth gospel is like an art gallery with a room of portraits of the same person all painted by one of the great masters.

John's work displays great depth perception—much of what he writes has deep connections to the Old Testament revelation. But he also has a genius for capturing the depth of character of the person he is portraying. His finished portraits are multidimensional. As we look at them, we see what is "there"—and yet there always seems to be more to see. John seems to be saying to us that if all the portraits needed to express the grace of Jesus were painted, all the art galleries in the world could not contain them![1]

That is true of this section. John's first portrait carries the title "Jesus the Savior." But beside it is another painting, of the same scene. It bears the title "Jesus the Example." As our Savior, He brings us the blessings of salvation. As our Example, He shows us the way to the blessings of a transformed life.

In Gethsemane and at Calvary, Jesus stepped down to bear our sin on His body on the tree (1 Peter 2:24). Later He emerged from the tomb, resurrected. And later still He ascended to glory. The message of the acted parable of the foot-washing was that the Lord of glory became the servant of sinners, took our shame, and now is Lord of all, exalted at the right hand of the Father.

But John's next portrait reflects Jesus' desire that His disciples (then and now) will see more—namely, how His acted parable carries implications for their lives.

Jesus had said to Peter: "What I am doing you do not understand now, but afterward you will understand" (John 13:7). Peter found Jesus' acted parable difficult to understand because he did not yet grasp the reality it represented. Later he would be able to say, "Oh, now I see! Jesus was showing us how He would become our Savior."

But now, having resumed His seat, the Master says to His disciples, "Do you understand what I have done?" (John 13:12).

Here it seems He expects them to be able to understand.

What explains this paradox?

John realized that in the foot-washing, the Lord Jesus was showing them two distinct but inseparable truths about Himself:

He was their Savior—although how He would accomplish their salvation they still did not understand.

But He was also their Example. They ought to be able to understand that, since He was their Lord, they were called to imitate Him.

Understand is a key term in the Christian's vocabulary.

Understanding What Jesus Christ Did

Jesus wants His disciples to understand the significance of what He came to do for them, and then to make connections between what He has done and what they are to do.

Understanding, the key to transformed Christian living, lies here—not primarily in our affections, or our emotions, or our instincts, or even our will. Christ will gradually transform all these. But He does so through our understanding of the gospel.

As its truth affects the way we think, it begins to change the way we feel; that in turn affects what we want, and the way we behave. Thus the gospel fuels the way we live.

This is the principle enunciated in Romans 12:1–2. The transformation of our lives takes place by means of the renewal of our minds.

But this familiar emphasis on the mind and understanding was not an invention of the Apostle Paul. The Lord Jesus emphasizes it here.

But what are we expected to understand? This: our Lord's rising from supper, washing the feet of His proud disciples, and then resuming His place is the basic model for the Christian lifestyle.

People often equate being a Christian with "living by the Golden Rule." Jesus did in fact teach a positive version of it: "As you wish that others would do to you, do so to them" (Luke 6:31). We should love our neighbors as ourselves. But Jesus is not giving us a lecture on ethics here. His Golden Rule is not a piece of moral advice disconnected from Himself. It is modeled by Him, and the power to follow it is found only in Him.

Here, in the upper room, we see the connection: because the disciples have a "share" with Him as their Savior, He is the "double cure" from sin's "guilt and power."[2] As a result, they are not only to do for others what they would like them to do for themselves. Nor for that matter are they only to do for others more than they expect others to do for them! They are to do for others what the Lord Jesus was willing to do for them—and become their servants for His sake!

So, the issue for me as a Christian is not: "How would I like them to treat me? Then I should try to do the same for them."

Instead it is: "How has the Lord Jesus treated me? Then that is the model for the way I will treat others. With His help I will display the same grace He has shown to me!" These moments in the upper room left an indelible impression on Simon Peter. He had, of course, a front-row seat. He may even have been the first disciple whose feet Jesus washed. He was certainly the first (and perhaps the only one) to protest. But writing later to fellow believers scattered throughout the Roman Empire, he urged them, "Clothe yourselves, all of you, with humility toward one another" (1 Peter 5:5).

The Greek verb for "clothe" used here (*egkomboomai*) reflects the picture of a slave tying a towel around his waist, just as Jesus had done. Our calling, shared with every Christian, is to see how and where and to whom we can serve as bondservants.

Jesus was giving the Apostles an "example" (Greek *hupodeigma*) to follow (John 13:15). Peter also says that Jesus left "an example" (1 Peter 2:21) but uses a different word (Greek *hupogrammos*). We might be able to guess its origin, since it contains the word for a letter (Greek *grammos*, from which words such as *grammar* are derived). The picture behind *hupogrammos* is that of a child learning to write. The teacher writes a word or sentence, and the child then copies it. It is as if Peter is saying: "Jesus wrote the book on lifestyle; copy it; write your story with an eye to the way He wrote His story." This is what the Holy Spirit helps us do—to become more like Jesus, producing in us the same servant disposition.

When the example of Jesus is fixed in our minds—as it became fixed in the mind of Peter—as we begin to understand the significance of what Jesus has done, we will begin instinctively to follow His example and become "copies" of His life. That is what it means to be Christlike.

Understanding Who Jesus Christ Is

There is a further dimension to notice here: the importance of who Jesus is. The significance of this foot-washing lies in the fact that it was done by the Lord of glory, the King of heaven, the Son of the Living God, the Word who was face-to-face with God.

When we understand who has humbled Himself for us, it changes everything. Respond to Him in faith and love, and deep instincts of humility and grace are the fruit. If the Lord of glory did this for me, nothing will hinder me from following His example. I will learn from my Master. How proud I have been! If He, the King of glory, washed disciples' dirty feet, then I will also be willing and eager to wash the dirt from the feet of others. Logic demands it.

An Empty Space in the Portrait Gallery

If we imagine the events that took place in the upper room as a series of portraits of Jesus, a painting seems to be missing. There is a space alongside the twin portraits of "Jesus the Savior" and "Jesus the Example." There is no portrait "Jesus Kneels before His Betrayer." Perhaps John could not bear to paint it.

You can guess the missing scene. John says nothing about it. Perhaps he felt it was one thing to paint the Lord Jesus kneeling before Peter knowing full well that he would deny Him. But how could he portray "Jesus washes the feet of Judas"? All he does is describe the foot-washing in a way that makes clear that before Judas left on his errand of betrayal, Jesus knelt down in front of him, too, and washed his feet.

Jesus had explained to the disciples the significance of the words in Psalm 41:9: "[He] who ate my bread, has lifted his heel against me." One of them would betray Him. But knowing that the Master's betrayal was a fulfillment of prophecy would surely help stabilize them later (John 13:19). The Father's sovereign purposes were not being disrupted by Satan. In fact, Jesus had long known that it was an integral part of His plan.

But Jesus knew not only that He would be betrayed. He knew His betrayer's identity—Judas Iscariot. It was in full knowledge of this that He knelt down and removed the grime from his feet.

This picture is absent from John's word-portrait gallery. It is implied in John 13:30 (Judas left the room after the foot-washing) but not described. Yet it adds to the challenge of Jesus' words, "I have given you an example, that you also should do just as I have done to you" (John 13:15). There are no exceptions to the feet we are called to wash. Every natural instinct that cries out "but not his" or "not hers" is suffocated by Christ's love for us and in us and by our desire to imitate Him. This is implicit in the mission on which Christ sends the Apostles. And, as He explains, if people will receive their ministry in His name, then they will also receive Him (13:20).

Challenging although this may be, there is nothing complex or complicated about it (we are the ones who are complex and complicated!). What Jesus did is described in simple sentences. He got up from supper. He took off His outer clothes. He put on the servant's towel. He filled a basin with water. He knelt down. He washed His disciples' dirty feet. He put on His clothes. He returned to His seat at the table. Imitating Him is not rocket science but simply a matter of humility and love and of following His example.

What enables us to do this?

First, as Jesus urges us, we need to understand the significance of who He is and what He has done for us. We too may have denied Him and perhaps, in the past, even betrayed Him. If Jesus has taken the servant's role for us, should we not do the same for others?

But there is another lesson for us here. We need to understand who Jesus is and what He has done in order to understand who we now are.

Understanding Who We Are in Jesus Christ

Our identity as Christians—as "Christ's ones"—is determined by and grows out of what Jesus did and who Jesus is. He says, "I then, your Lord and Teacher, . . . have given you an example, that you also should do just as I have done to you." This does not mean that we should inaugurate a sacrament of foot-washing in the church.[3] No, this is an example. And we are called to give concrete expression to it because of another principle: "You call me Teacher and Lord, and you are right, for so I am. . . . Truly, truly, I say to you, a servant is not greater than his master, nor is a messenger greater than the one who sent him" (John 13:13, 16).

This is one of Jesus' "Amen, amen" sayings.

When we write something, we have various ways to express emphasis. A couple of actions on a keyboard can underline words, or make them stand out in bold print, or change their font into italic script. In this way we tell the reader visually, "This is important."

In Hebrew literature, this kind of emphasis was expressed by repetition. The first example in the Bible is in Genesis 2:17: "Of the tree of the knowledge of good and evil you shall not eat, for in the day that you eat of it you shall surely die." The use of "surely" here in our English translation emphasizes the warning—"Believe

Me, this really will happen; it is not an idle threat. Take My words seriously." The way the Hebrew Bible expresses this is by saying "dying you shall die." The verb is repeated for the sake of emphasis. Perhaps it reminds you of a warning your schoolteacher (or father!) gave you—"I have told you twice already . . . !"

Everything Jesus says is important. Everything He says is the Word of God. But on a number of occasions, He indicates that what He is saying is especially important by introducing His words with "Amen, amen"—"Truly, truly, I say to you."

What, then, is so significant for us here?

If He is my Teacher, then I am His pupil and will seek to learn from Him.

If He is my Lord, then as His servant I will seek to represent Him well.

If we understand these two principles, we will begin to think about ourselves in new ways. Our "self-image" will change. We will see ourselves now as disciples and bondservants of the Lord Jesus. Our mind is to be instructed by His teaching; our will is to do the will of our Master. We will take to heart what Paul says: "You are not your own, for you were bought with a price. So glorify God in your body" (1 Cor. 6:19–20).

We Are Bondservants of Christ

"I am no longer my own" is a first principle of the Christian life. As the Heidelberg Catechism puts it: "I with body and soul, both in life and death, am not my own, but belong to my faithful Savior Jesus Christ; who, with his precious blood, has fully satisfied for all my sins."[4]

That really is a new self-image, isn't it? Jesus did not come to top-up your life or to help you get it better organized. He owns you. He came to make you a happy bond-slave who has discovered that his "service is perfect freedom."[5] Now, at last, we learn to pray:

Make me a captive, Lord,
And then I shall be free.
Force me to render up my sword,
And I shall conqueror be.

My will is not my own
Till thou hast made it thine;
If it would reach a monarch's throne,
It must its crown resign.[6]

A staff member at a wedding reception at which I was a guest dropped an entire tray, full of dishes, near the table at which I was sitting. The rest of the staff simply went on with their tasks. Surprised, I turned to the close friend seated beside me and said (in a moment of folly), "Somebody should help her!"

"Well?" he said.

He only needed one word! I got the point, got up, and tried to help.

My friend had (quite rightly) challenged my assumption: "Somebody (else), somebody on the staff, should do something." The implication was really, "Somebody (else) should humble themselves to help her."

Was my Lord Jesus also thinking, "Well? Have you forgotten who you are?"

We all encounter situations, whether major or trivial, that require self-humbling if we are to serve Christ in them. The same is true—sometimes more so—with difficult people, pain-in-the-neck-type people. We think, even if we do not say: "Why should I serve them? Kneel down before them? They don't deserve it."

But Simon Peter didn't "deserve it." Judas Iscariot didn't "deserve it." No indeed. And we didn't "deserve it" either. But the Son of God stooped down to lift us up; He washed away the dirt of our sin; He bought us with His blood. We are not our own now, but His. And when we begin to see this clearly, we learn to think like Paul: "We were ready to share with you not only the gospel of God but also our own selves" (1 Thess. 2:8); we are "your servants [or bondservants] for Jesus' sake" (2 Cor. 4:5).

Bondservants—that is who we are now.

Not so long ago, *sacrifice* and *service* were among the first words young Christians learned. They featured prominently in books about the Christian life. But it is rare today to see a Christian book, hear a sermon, or attend a conference with the word *sacrifice* in the title. By contrast, we are inundated with teaching about how the gospel improves our lives or solves our problems, not how it calls us to sacrifice and turns us into bondservants. Many Christian youngsters are led to believe that they are being trained to be "tomorrow's leaders." In fact, the word *leader* rarely appears in the New Testament. We have lost sight of the Teacher whose gospel trains us to be "today's bondservants." We need to have our thinking profoundly recalibrated.

We Are Also Disciples of Our Master and Therefore His Representatives

We are called to give visible expression to Jesus' teaching. People inevitably form their views of the Lord Jesus from our lives—we are, after all, "Christ's-ones." The impression they have of Him they gain from us. Jesus spells out this principle in another "Truly, truly" saying: "Whoever receives the one I send receives me, and whoever receives me receives the one who sent me" (John 13:20).

In the elementary school I attended, a crate of milk bottles was brought into the classroom every morning. Lessons were suspended while every pupil engaged in the daily ritual of drinking a third of a pint of milk! I later read that Japanese people thought that "Scottish people smell like milk." Hardly surprising. If you are not from a nation of milk drinkers, I imagine your olfactory senses are sensitive to people who are drinking several pints of it every week! In a similar way, nonsmokers sense immediately when someone who has been smoking gets into the elevator—although the smoker may be completely oblivious to the odor that surrounds him.

There is a spiritual parallel. We all leave an aroma behind us when we exit a room. People notice the "atmosphere" of our lives; they comment on it behind our backs. That is especially true of Christians, because in most contexts we are in an obvious minority. But does "the aroma of Christ" linger when you leave?[7] Has your life been fragrant with His humility and grace? Did it say, however wordlessly, "I am Christ's bondservant, and therefore I want to serve you too"?

Challenging, yes. But listen again to the Master: "If you know these things, blessed are you if you do them" (John 13:17).

That is not rocket science either, is it?

Here, then, is a spiritual health-check: Before whom did I last inwardly kneel and say, "I am your servant for Jesus' sake"?

So, we are to understand what Christ has done and who He is. We are also to understand who we are—His bondservants and disciples. But before we leave this section, there is a further element to notice in Jesus' teaching.

Understanding the Way of Blessing

"If you know these things," Jesus says, "blessed are you if you do them" (John 13:17).

In Scripture, "blessing" is a key idea with a varied vocabulary. Its presence runs from Genesis 1:22 to Revelation 22:14. Its foundation lies in God's covenant love for His people and His purposes to bring them true happiness. Its opposite is the "cursing" that characterizes life lived apart from and in antagonism toward God—life that declines into dysfunction, barrenness, disintegration, and ultimately death.

The New Testament uses two different Greek words that our English versions translate as "blessed": *euologētos* ("well spoken of"—God is "blessed," i.e., we "speak well" of Him in our praises; we are "blessed," i.e., He "speaks well" of us in His grace) and *makarios* ("happy," "fortunate"; the word used here and in the Beatitudes, Matt. 5:1–12).

In both Matthew's record of the Sermon on the Mount and John's record of the upper room, Jesus is describing the blessed (*makarios*) life of the disciple. In both contexts, He indicates that there is something counterintuitive about it; the way up to it is actually the way down. It involves being set free from our obsession with ourselves and the merely temporal and learning to open our hands to God, allowing everything that we have held too tightly to drop out of them. We can then receive Christ and every spiritual blessing in Him with both hands. The effect is that we become increasingly like Him.

Jesus is teaching the disciples a vital principle. Understanding is important. Knowledge is essential. But blessing does not come merely from knowing or even from understanding. It comes from obeying, from putting what we understand into practice. There is blessing that we never experience so long as we insist on standing on our own dignity. But we will experience it if we are willing to kneel down and serve those who do not deserve the grace of the Lord Jesus Christ.

And who does deserve it? Certainly not us!

The point? The way of blessing is a servant way—not just for its own sake or for the sake of others but for God's sake.

Jesus chose this way—it was the ultimate countercultural action, the Lord of glory washing His disciples' dirty feet (what did His angels think He was doing?).

What, then, does it mean to understand Him and to follow Him?

It means not standing on our dignity but taking a servant's towel.

It means not standing at all but being willing to kneel.

It means not standing apart but doing the humble and the menial tasks.

It means being willing to do the slave-like thing—for Jesus' sake.

We should never forget that the Lord Jesus was willing to wash the heel that was lifted up to crush Him.

3
—

From Trouble to Glory

John 13:21–31

After saying these things, Jesus was troubled in his spirit, and testified, "Truly, truly, I say to you, one of you will betray me." The disciples looked at one another, uncertain of whom he spoke. One of his disciples, whom Jesus loved, was reclining at table at Jesus' side, so Simon Peter motioned to him to ask Jesus of whom he was speaking. So that disciple, leaning back against Jesus, said to him, "Lord, who is it?" Jesus answered, "It is he to whom I will give this morsel of bread when I have dipped it." So when he had dipped the morsel, he gave it to Judas, the son of Simon Iscariot. Then after he had taken the morsel, Satan entered into him. Jesus said to him, "What you are going to do, do quickly." Now no one at the table knew why he said this to him. Some thought that, because Judas had the moneybag, Jesus was telling him, "Buy what we need for the feast," or that he should give something to the poor. So, after receiving the morsel of bread, he immediately went out. And it was night.

When he had gone out, Jesus said, "Now is the Son of Man glorified, and God is glorified in him."

S omething significant happens in the upper room in the short period of time that John describes in a mere eleven verses (John 13:21–31). The atmosphere changes dramatically: "After saying these things, Jesus was troubled in his spirit, and testified, 'Truly, truly, I say to you, one of you will betray me'" (v. 21). But then, a few verses later, "Jesus said, 'Now is the Son of Man glorified, and God is glorified in him'" (v. 31).

What happened to change the atmosphere? "Judas . . . went out."

One of the motifs running through John's gospel is that of light and dark.[1] So he almost certainly intends a double entendre when he says that "it was night." But the night had already been inside the room, in the heart of Judas. When he leaves, the room seems to flood with light. Now John's record takes us to the very heart of who Christ is and what He has come to do.

The most famous painting in my home city's art gallery is not its Rembrandt or its Van Gogh but Salvador Dalí's *Christ of St. John of the Cross*. It is a massive—some seven feet by four feet—intensely dramatic representation of Christ on the cross.

What is arresting about Dalí's portrayal is that the spectator's view is from above; we are looking down on the back of Christ's muscular upper body and bowed head. His face is hidden from us. And the cross seems to be floating on a dark sky (toward us? or away from us?). It hovers over a stretch of water by the shore of which a fishing boat lies anchored.

Many liberal theologians' portrayals of Christ seem to be little more than maximized versions of their own world-and-life-view. Something similar is true of Dalí's representation of Him. He said that his inspiration was a "cosmic dream." His Christ epitomizes a worldview: Christ for him was "the very unity of the universe."

Most visitors to the gallery are not art critics (who have always been divided on the merits of Dalí's painting). I suspect many spectators assume that the reference in the painting's title is to the Apostle John. But Dalí's Christ is not the Christ of John's gospel.[2] There are no wounds on the strong body, no scourge marks on the shoulders, no blood. I remember as a student reading some comments on the painting by Francis Schaeffer. He made the simple but important observation that in Dalí's representation the cross never touches the earth. Perhaps this is why Dalí's title refers to a Spanish mystic, John of the Cross (1542–91).

But the Christ of John's gospel is not a mystical figure; He is the Word made flesh, living in our world, experiencing our pain, despised and rejected, and bearing our sin. In the upper room, He is burdened by the knowledge that one of His closest associates, the treasurer of His disciple band, would betray Him; and beyond that He is already conscious of the suffering He will endure and the accompanying sense of God-forsakenness.

This is the Christ of John the Evangelist.

John has just recorded our Lord's exhortation to the Apostles to follow His example. But now he seems to pause the action for a moment so that we can reflect on the costliness of the reality to which the Savior's acted parable has pointed.

Jesus now clarifies His earlier reference to Psalm 41: "One of you will betray me" (John 13:21). A ripple of "Is it I?" went around the table (see Matt. 26:22; Mark 14:19).

Peter, now more composed, nodded to John (who was next to Jesus)—you can almost see him mouthing the words—"Ask Him who it is." He does. Jesus responds: "It is the one to whom I will give this piece of bread, once I have dipped it."

John watched as the sop was handed to Judas Iscariot.

Troubled in Spirit

No wonder "Jesus was troubled in his spirit" (John 13:21). In contexts such as this, the verb John uses (Greek *tarassō*) means being agitated, perplexed, or shaken up. It is one of several terms the Gospel writers use to describe the turmoil Jesus experienced that night. It is a strong term—although not the strongest, for there is more to come.

The other Gospels use similar language, especially of Jesus' experience in the garden of Gethsemane. There He has a kind of profound homesickness as He contemplates drinking the cup of divine judgment.[3]

Reflect on the word "troubled" for a moment. It may ring a bell. A few verses further on, Jesus, who here is "troubled," will tell His disciples not to "be troubled" (14:1). John uses the same verb in both cases. Is there a connection? We will need to reflect on that later.

In the immediate context, Jesus is troubled in spirit because His betrayer is present in the room.

One person in a room can spoil the whole atmosphere. So here, the deep sensitivity of Jesus' spirit was grieved by the presence of Judas.

How could Judas be willing to betray Jesus? He had been with Jesus for three years, heard Him preach countless times, seen His miracles of compassion and power, professed to be His disciple. He had even been appointed to the trusted post of treasurer of the Apostolic band. Yet he harbored a resentment against the Lord Jesus. This must have troubled the Savior's heart for some time. Now it had reached a point of inner distress.

Even at this late stage, the disciples cannot understand what is actually happening.

By contrast, as readers of John's gospel, we have already been given hints that we should keep our eye on Judas Iscariot.[4]

Betrayer Revealed

From as early as John 6:71, we have known that Judas will betray his Lord.

We also learn that he was pilfering money from the disciples' treasury (John 12:4–6). When Jesus was anointed with expensive perfume by a grateful Mary of Bethany, Judas had murmured: "This ointment was worth a year's wages. It could have been sold and we could have used the money to help the poor." What he really meant was that he could have used the money himself. Yet he seems to have been trusted implicitly—so much so that when Jesus told him, "What you are going to do, do quickly," everybody assumed he was either going to buy something related to the feast or going to engage in some mercy ministry at Passover time (13:29).

So, how did Jesus know about Judas?

First of all, He knew somebody would betray Him. It was written in the Scriptures: "[He] who ate my bread, has lifted his heel against me" (Ps. 41:9). Is that expression "lifted his heel against me" deliberately reminiscent of the promise of Genesis 3:15 that the serpent would crush the heel of the Savior? It is as though, in seeking to crush the Savior, the evil one would, as it were, miss His head and catch Him only on the heel. Jesus knew the Hebrew Bible. He knew that there was a strand of prophecy running from Genesis 3:15 through Psalm 41:9 and beyond that would be fulfilled in Him.

But how did Jesus know that the prophecy would be fulfilled by Judas Iscariot in particular?

We might say: "Well, of course He knew it was Judas Iscariot. Jesus was God after all." But in the Gospels, Jesus characteristically discerns God's purposes from the Scriptures and by the help the Holy Spirit gave Him to interpret and apply them to Himself. He also—as John says earlier—knew what was in people (John 2:24–25). He knew Scripture, and He knew Judas—and drew His own conclusion.

This is spiritual discernment. Sometimes we, too, "sense" things about people—for example, whether we can trust them. We might not be able to put into words exactly what we feel, but we are aware that there are some people we cannot fully trust. If this is true of ourselves, who experience the desensitizing effects of sin, then we can appreciate that our sinless Savior had a far greater sensitivity to who people really were. He is the Word of God "discerning the thoughts and intentions of the heart. . . . All are naked and exposed to the eyes of him to whom we must give account" (Heb. 4:12–13). He could discern the telltale signs of

Judas' distancing himself from Him. He saw his spirit of "anti-grace": Judas saw Jesus being gracious to Mary and was repelled rather than attracted (John 12:1–8).

We tend to assume that when people see love in action, they will respond positively. But with the love of Jesus, that is far from true. Perhaps you know that. You saw the grace of Christ in someone's life, or in the gospel story—but you actually hated it, ran from it, and sought to protect yourself against it, or perhaps you demeaned the person in whose life you saw and felt Christ's presence.

So, the grace that saves and that is present in others' lives serves as a kind of litmus test of where we really are spiritually. However counterintuitive it may seem, in this respect by nature people prefer law to grace. They think they can keep the law—if they set their minds to it, and they can compensate for any past faults by promising to "do better."

But you cannot "do" grace. Accepting God's grace is an indication that you realize there is nothing you can do to compensate.

People also think of the law as impersonal, controllable, manageable. But the Lord Jesus—who is the grace of God—is more personal and more challenging. With Him it is not a matter of doing better but of acknowledging our helplessness and asking for His saving grace. That is humbling. And so even people who are conscious that they have broken God's law, whose lives have become distorted, even people racked with guilt or shame—refuse grace.

Judas must have been like that. He saw grace in Jesus' life and heard it in His words. But he refused that grace and reacted against it. What repelled Judas and sent him headlong into his betrayal was "the grace of the Lord Jesus Christ" (2 Cor. 13:14)!

A minister once told me about a physician who telephoned him in great distress. He agreed to meet her for coffee in a local hotel (a practice ministers would be ill-advised to follow today). She told him her story and explained what was troubling her. He responded simply, "Have you ever asked for forgiveness?" She became angry, picked up her belongings, and stomped out of the hotel. She had wanted to be told how to heal herself. But she refused the medicine that could pardon her sins and deliver her from guilt. Rather than trust in what Someone Else had done, she wanted to claw her way back from her guilt by her own efforts. She balked at saying:

Not the labors of my hands
can fulfill thy law's demands;
could my zeal no respite know,
could my tears forever flow,
all for sin could not atone;
thou must save, and thou alone.

Nothing in my hand I bring,
simply to thy cross I cling;
naked, come to thee for dress;
helpless, look to thee for grace;
foul, I to the Fountain fly;
wash me, Savior, or I die.[5]

There are times when the very mention of the grace of forgiveness in Jesus Christ simply stimulates an inner hostility.

So it must have been with Judas, even if, in his case, he had become well practiced in masking it.

When Jesus began to unmask him and indicated that He knew

his dark secret, did Judas join in with the other disciples and ask, "Lord, is it I?"—perhaps just a second behind them—or did he remain tight-lipped and silent? He must have been relieved to leave the room. Now he needed to see Jesus only once more—to identify Him by the signal of the betraying kiss. Perhaps the last straw for him had been seeing His grace as He washed his dirty feet. Did he look away from the eyes of the kneeling Savior? Or did his steely gaze say: "How dare You! How dare You place Your hands of grace on my feet?"

Some Christians feel uncomfortable at the thought that Jesus washed Judas' feet. Surely Jesus didn't, couldn't, do that? Not Judas' feet!

Does this reflect the fact that there are dirty feet they themselves would never wash?

Judas was unwilling to receive Christ. Ultimately, he valued Him worth no more than a slave. Tragically, he is the clearest illustration in the New Testament of the words of Hebrews: "It is impossible, in the case of those who have once been enlightened, who have tasted the heavenly gift, and have shared in the Holy Spirit, and have tasted the goodness of the word of God and the powers of the age to come, and then have fallen away, to restore them again to repentance, since they are crucifying once again the Son of God to their own harm and holding him up to contempt" (Heb. 6:4–6).

Jesus had been troubled in spirit. He had revealed His betrayer. And as He passed the sop to Judas Iscariot, He settled His destiny.

Settled Destiny

At this stage in the gospel narrative, Jesus is already victimized by Judas. Soon the temple guard and the Jewish leaders will join in.

They will be followed by Roman soldiers who will debase Him. He will be mocked, struck, spat upon, scourged, and crucified. Together, the religious and secular authorities will conspire to destroy Him.

But none of these individuals or groups, nor all of them together, has the authority or power to settle Jesus' destiny— although, without exception, they believe they hold it in their hands. At every stage, it is Jesus Himself who is in control of His situation. Now, as His Father's plan is coming to its crisis point, He dismisses Judas to do his work. In essence, He says, "What you are going to do, you will do now according to My Father's plan and under His sovereign control; and this will therefore be ultimately for My glory and for the salvation of the world." As Martin Luther said, "The devil is God's devil."

Here, then, is Judas Iscariot. And behind him lurks the evil one seeking to destroy Jesus. He knows, however, that this will not lead to His destruction. The serpent will strike His heel; but that struck heel will crush the serpent's head. Victory will be His.

This is why, when Judas leaves the room, the atmosphere changes. It becomes cleaner. The darkness outside cannot destroy the glory that is emerging inside.

4
—
Atmospheric Changes

John 13:31–38

When he had gone out, Jesus said, "Now is the Son of Man glorified, and God is glorified in him. If God is glorified in him, God will also glorify him in himself, and glorify him at once. Little children, yet a little while I am with you. You will seek me, and just as I said to the Jews, so now I also say to you, 'Where I am going you cannot come.' A new commandment I give to you, that you love one another: just as I have loved you, you also are to love one another. By this all people will know that you are my disciples, if you have love for one another."

Simon Peter said to him, "Lord, where are you going?" Jesus answered him, "Where I am going you cannot follow me now, but you will follow afterward." Peter said to him, "Lord, why can I not follow you now? I will lay down my life for you." Jesus answered, "Will you lay down your life for me? Truly, truly, I say to you, the rooster will not crow till you have denied me three times."

T he curtain is now coming down on Act 1 of the drama of the upper room. We have already begun to see the truth of Calvin's statement that John's gospel shows us Christ's soul.

The atmosphere in the upper room keeps changing. Questions and answers, pride and humility, shame and joy, betrayal and faithfulness are all here.

But now Judas has left the room. For Jesus, there is no turning back from the cross. And yet, at least in some measure, He seems relieved. Now only those who are "clean" surround Him (John 13:10; 15:3). The dark heart among them has now left for the night outside (13:30). The room feels brighter, the atmosphere seems cleaner, even easier. Jesus senses it, and explains why to the disciples: "Now is the Son of man glorified, and God is glorified in him" (v. 31).

The die is cast. Jesus has crossed a Rubicon.[1] Now there is no turning back. The passion agony still awaits Him. It is now irreversible, but He is conscious of "the joy that was set before him." Here it seems to flood His soul, even if there still awaits Him the shame He must despise (Heb. 12:2).

Glorified

Jesus' language is now so different that the disciples must have sensed that something had changed. Only minutes ago, He had been troubled in spirit. But now He is speaking about His glorification. A crisis point has been reached and passed. It is not the last one He will face, but a burden has fallen from His shoulders, the point of no return has been passed. Now the way, however dark, is clear.

Earlier in His ministry Jesus had refrained from doing "mighty works" in Nazareth "because of their unbelief" (Matt. 13:58). It would have been inappropriate. He would only have been throwing pearls to pigs, to use His own expression (7:6). Here in the upper room there was a similar restraint. He had refrained from opening His heart fully so long as Judas the unbeliever was still present. But now that the traitor has been banished from His presence, He does so; there are secrets He can share. It would indeed have been inappropriate for the Savior to "give dogs what is holy" (7:6).

Jesus speaks, therefore, in different tones: "Now is the Son of Man glorified, and God is glorified in him. If God is glorified in him, God will also glorify him in himself, and glorify him at once" (John 13:31–32).

This is the moment we have been waiting for since the beginning of John's gospel. It had been promised in the prologue: "The Word became flesh . . . and we have seen his glory, glory as of the only Son from the Father, full of grace and truth" (John 1:14). There had been a glimpse of that glory in the first week of His public ministry when Jesus had turned water into wine (2:11). John had hinted that it would later be seen in greater measure when he wrote that "the Spirit had not been given, because Jesus was not yet glorified" (7:39). And later still, when Lazarus died, Jesus had spoken about his death as a catalyst for the revelation of His glory (11:4). In one sense, He revealed that glory by raising Lazarus. But a fuller revelation was still to come. For that event would prompt the religious leaders to seek His death and would lead eventually to His crucifixion (11:43–53; 12:9–11). This—although the disciples could not yet grasp it—was the prelude to His resurrection glory.

Thus, in John's gospel, Jesus' glorification begins with His being "lifted up" on the cross. From there, He said, He would draw all people to Himself (12:32).

But what does the Savior mean when He talks about being glorified?

An important clue lies in the way He refers to Himself as being glorified as the Son of Man.

Jesus is the Son of God and the Son of Man—He is both divine and human. But there is more to the title Son of Man, for an obvious reason: with the single exception of Stephen (in Acts 7:56), Jesus Himself is the only person in the New Testament who ever uses it.

"Son of Man" can simply refer to "man" created to be the image of God and to serve Him (Ps. 8:4). God frequently addresses Ezekiel as "son of man" (Ezek. 2:1 and elsewhere). But it is also the title given to a figure who appears in the vision of Daniel 7:9–14:

"As I looked,

thrones were placed,
    and the Ancient of Days took his seat;
his clothing was white as snow,
    and the hair of his head like pure wool;
his throne was fiery flames;
    its wheels were burning fire.
A stream of fire issued
    and came out from before him;

a thousand thousands served him,

and ten thousand times ten thousand stood before him;
the court sat in judgment,

and the books were opened.

"I looked then because of the sound of the great words that the horn was speaking. And as I looked, the beast was killed, and its body destroyed and given over to be burned with fire. As for the rest of the beasts, their dominion was taken away, but their lives were prolonged for a season and a time.

"I saw in the night visions,

and behold, with the clouds of heaven
there came one like a son of man,
and he came to the Ancient of Days
and was presented before him.
And to him was given dominion
and glory and a kingdom,
that all peoples, nations, and languages
should serve him;
his dominion is an everlasting dominion,
which shall not pass away,
and his kingdom one
that shall not be destroyed. . . .

" 'And the kingdom and the dominion
and the greatness of the kingdoms under the whole
heaven

shall be given to the people of the saints of the Most High;
his kingdom shall be an everlasting kingdom,
and all dominions shall serve and obey him."
(Dan. 7:9–14, 27)

This son of man ascends triumphantly to the throne of the
Ancient of Days; the enemies "the beast" and "the rest of the
beasts"—are defeated. As victor he shares the spoils of his triumph
with the saints of the Most High. He is given universal dominion
and rules over it without end.

In fact, this scene has deep roots running back through Psalm
8 to the garden of Eden. God created man, male and female, as His
image—to reflect His character in miniature form and to exercise
dominion over the earth in a way that mirrored God's dominion
over all creation. But the fall brought all this to a disastrous end.

What Daniel sees is a fragment of the story of how God will
bring about a glorious reversal and restoration through the incarnation, ministry, death, resurrection, and ascension of the Lord
Jesus Christ.

As Jesus meditated on the promise of Genesis 3:15, He
realized that in the Old Testament the Seed of the woman was
portrayed by means of several different figures: the Priest after
the order of Melchizedek, the Prophet like Moses, the King like
David, the Suffering Servant prophesied by Isaiah—and also the
Son of Man portrayed in Daniel's vision. All these figures would
merge in one person—Jesus Himself. His multidimensional work
needed to be described in a multiperson way.

So, while the title Son of Man certainly refers to our Lord's
humanity—and His humiliation as the Suffering Servant—it

particularly has in view His exaltation at the right hand of the Father. It refers to the expansion of His kingdom after His conflict with and defeat of His enemy. He would exercise "dominion," because as a result of His victory "all authority in heaven and on earth" would be His (Matthew 28:18 very clearly echoes Daniel 7:14, which in turn clearly echoes Psalm 8:6, which in turn then echoes Genesis 1:28).

What was not clear in Daniel's vision, although there are hints of it in the reference to the beasts, was that the ascent of the Son of Man would take place via His descent into a world in bondage to the powers of darkness and His victory over them. The Son of Man was also the Suffering Servant. The Priest who entered the presence of God carried His own sacrificial blood; the King's coronation throne lies at the end of the Via Dolorosa.

So, when Jesus says that "the time has come for the Son of Man to be glorified," all this is in view. And even when He is demeaned by Caiaphas, He is comforted by the "joy that was set before him" (Heb. 12:2) and knows that as the Son of Man He will soon be "at the right hand of Power and coming on the clouds of heaven" (Matt. 26:64). The "coming" here then, since it echoes Daniel 7:13–14, may well refer not only to Christ's second coming in glory but also to His going to the Father to receive glory.

All this Jesus had already illustrated in the earlier foot-washing. His kneeling was the preamble to His reigning and His shame the forerunner of His glory.

Jesus will be glorified as the Son of Man, and His Father will be glorified in His obedience.

This point is made regularly in John's gospel. Jesus was conscious that the Father had sent Him; His calling was to live by

His Father's timetable (John 2:4; 7:6, 8, 30; 8:20; 12:23, 27; 13:1). His becoming "obedient to the point of death, even death on a cross" (Phil. 2:8) demonstrated how great His heavenly Father must be to be worthy of an obedience that had no limitations placed on it.

So, there is a twofold glorification here: the Son is to be glorified by the Father and the Father is being glorified by the Son.

But how is God going to glorify the Son of Man "at once" (John 13:32)?

Part of the answer is that Jesus' crucifixion will soon be followed by His resurrection when He will be "declared to be the Son of God in power according to the Spirit of holiness by his resurrection from the dead" (Rom. 1:4).

But more is implied.

Jesus will be tried, condemned, and summarily executed as a criminal. Yet the gospel writers indicate a paradox that occurs at every stage of this process: Jesus' accusers acknowledge that He is not guilty. The Sanhedrin cannot make their charges stick and their witnesses contradict each other; Pilate can find no fault in Him; the crowd baying for His execution cannot prove Him guilty; a condemned criminal recognizes that "this man has done nothing wrong" (Luke 23:41); even the centurion in charge of His execution squad confesses, "Truly this man was the Son of God!" (Mark 15:39).

This repeated confession of His innocence runs through the accounts of Jesus' passion like a coded message. Those who condemned Him become the mouthpiece of another verdict that will be publicly announced by God in His resurrection. Then His perfect sinlessness and complete obedience will be made known.

Then He will be raised to life by the glory of the Father to share in His glory (Rom. 6:4).

What is the key to this coded message? Why is it that everybody who tries Him declares Him to be innocent, yet participates in His condemnation and death? Death is the wages of sin (Rom. 6:23). But if Jesus is not dying for His own sins, for whose sins is He dying? Asking the question in this way elicits the New Testament's answer: "In Christ God was . . . not counting their trespasses against them. . . . For our sake he made him to be sin who knew no sin, so that in him we might become the righteousness of God" (2 Cor. 5:19, 21).

> And can it be that I should gain
> An interest in the Savior's blood?
> Died he for me, who caused his pain—
> For me, who him to death pursued?
> Amazing love! How can it be
> That thou, my God, shouldst die for me?[2]

If we follow the logic of John's gospel, we see the crucifixion of Jesus not as an event that evokes a sentimental sadness but as the beginning of His glorification. Even Pilate's inscription fixed to the cross proclaimed Him to be "Jesus of Nazareth, the King . . ." in the three languages of the ancient Near East and the Roman Empire—Aramaic, Latin, and Greek (John 19:19–20). The glory of His true identity would emerge in fuller measure in His resurrection and ascension, and then in the outpouring of the Holy Spirit on the day of Pentecost. It will ultimately be displayed when He comes again in power in the resurrection of the last day. But it had already begun at the cross.

As a result of Jesus' bearing our sins, the cross has become the irrefutable proof of God's love for us (Rom. 5:8). Christ crucified has brought the forgiveness of sins and new life to all who believe and has inaugurated the calling of the worldwide and eternity-long family of God. All this is to the glory of the Son. The early fathers of the church used to say that Christ extended His arms on the cross so that He might embrace people from every tribe and tongue, every people group and nation, to the ends of the earth and to the last day of history. The facts that you have this book in your hands today, and are thinking about John's gospel, and reading about Christ's salvation, are all indications that God has begun to glorify His Son throughout the earth. We are His Father's reward to Him for all that He has done for us.

This, then, is how Jesus viewed things. There is glory in the cross. He is not the victim there, but the Victor.

Yes, a dark cloud will soon come again upon the Savior's spirit. He will be prostrated in the garden of Gethsemane. He will thirst and cry out on the cross of Calvary. But here He was reassuring His disciples of what He Himself had long known. There was a reality deeper than the agony of Gethsemane and Calvary.

In later years, John would recall another enigmatic statement Jesus had made earlier: "For this reason the Father loves me, because I lay down my life that I may take it up again" (John 10:17).

Far from His substitutionary death being "child abuse"—as has been claimed, with a breathtaking ignoring of both Scripture and the entire history of Christian theology—the cross is the high point of the love of this Father and Son.

Thus, during the darkness of Gethsemane, and the agony of Calvary, it would have been possible for the Father to sing:

My Jesus, I love thee,
I know thou art mine; . . .
If ever I loved thee, my Jesus, 'tis now.[3]

But for the moment, Jesus is given a clear, if momentary, sense of the joy that is set before Him. And this will enable Him to endure the cross and despise the shame. He knows that this is the route to the throne.

For generations now, Scottish Presbyterians have sung Psalm 24:7–10 during communion services. Enshrined in it they have seen the ascension of Christ prefigured. They have imagined the triumphant Lord Jesus approaching the city of heavenly glory and His angelic retinue demanding entry for Him:

Ye gates, lift up your heads on high;
ye doors that last for aye,
be lifted up, that so the King
of glory enter may.

The guardian angels and archangels on heaven's ramparts respond with the great question:

But who of glory is the King?

And receive the answer:

The mighty Lord is this,
even that same Lord that great in might
and strong in battle is.

And so the command is repeated:

> Ye gates, lift up your heads; ye doors,
> doors that do last for aye,
> be lifted up, that so the King
> of glory enter may . . .
> Alleluia! alleluia!
> alleluia! alleluia! alleluia!
> Amen, amen, amen.[4]

In anticipation of that hour, the light of the Father's love for His Son floods the upper room. Sustained by that love, Jesus will be obedient in Gethsemane and at Calvary and during the long hours in between.

Change of Atmosphere—Again

Once more Jesus turns His attention to the disciples. Soon He will be parted from them, leaving them confused and desolate. For where He is going, they cannot come (John 13:33). In a moment He will speak words of comfort. But now He wants to impress on them the significance of what they have just witnessed: "A new commandment I give to you, that you love one another: just as I have loved you, you also are to love one another. By this all people will know that you are my disciples, if you have love for one another" (vv. 34–35).

What they have just seen and heard carries a simple implication: as Christ has shown His love to them, so they are to show it to one another. This is His "new commandment." As John elsewhere explains, it is not "new" in the sense of being "novel." It is the "old" commandment, to love God and to love our neighbor. But it is given new significance in its fulfillment in Jesus. He has shown that neighbor-love includes enemy-love. This is what makes it a "new commandment, . . . which is true in him and in you" (1 John 2:7–8). It did indeed come true in the disciples, so much so that the early theologian Tertullian could appeal to the testimony of pagans: "See how these Christians love one another" is a powerful apologetic for the gospel.[5]

But poor Simon Peter has not even heard this new commandment. All he can think about is Jesus' statement about leaving them. He cannot hide his reactions: "Where are you going? . . . Why can I not follow you now? I will lay down my life for you" (John 13:36–37).

Had he still not been listening? Or perhaps he had been, but Jesus' use of the past tense ("I have loved you") and the future tense ("All people will know") simply underlined Peter's sense of uncertainty about the present. He cannot contain himself. He must know where Jesus is going. And when he does, nothing on earth will stop him from following. And as for talking about loving each other, does Jesus not realize that he, Peter, loves Him more than life itself? He would lay down his life for Him. But he has no idea what He is saying.

And so, from hearing a few moments ago about the Father's glorifying the Lord Jesus, we are pitchforked into a different world where the weak mistakenly believes he is strong and the one who loves Jesus is told he will deny Him.

The mature Augustine of Hippo could write shrewdly, "I have become a puzzle to myself."[6] But Peter has no questions about himself. He is an immature disciple caught up into purposes of God that are far greater than he can understand. He mistakenly believes he knows himself and understands Jesus, but he still has not taken in what Jesus has repeatedly told him. His Master is going to be crucified. Did his mind simply refuse to take it in? Was that, at least in part, because of the unbearable implication—if Jesus were crucified, some of His blood would surely end up on Peter's clothes too?

So, Simon Peter still does not understand Jesus. He has been called to follow a crucified Savior. He continues to struggle to take that in. But neither does he understand himself, and so he blurts out that he is willing to die with Jesus, indeed instead of Him if need be!

We cannot share the fellowship of Christ's resurrection without sharing in the fellowship of His sufferings and being made like Him in His death (Phil. 3:10). Peter thought this was easier to understand than it actually is. Jesus tells him that he will have to walk the road of painful self-discovery first: "Will you lay down your life for me?" Now follows the fourth "Amen, amen" saying in this chapter: "Truly, truly, I say to you, the rooster will not crow till you have denied me three times" (John 13:38).

When John wrote his gospel, he did not include chapter divisions and verse numbers. Occasionally in the Bible these are less than helpful. But here the division is appropriate.

The chapter opens with the washing of Peter's feet; it closes with a challenge to Peter's life. It thus pinpoints the needs and the failures of a disciple who, notwithstanding, really did love his Lord. For such, Christ shed His precious blood. It was for the Simon Peters that He laid aside the garments of glory, stepped down into the world, became a servant, bore the burden of our sin, and rose and ascended in majesty and glory. It was so that Simon Peter and all those like him might join Him at the marriage supper of the Lamb. Our Lord's words would one day come true: "Peter, what I'm doing now you don't really understand. But the day will come when you will understand."

Peter did come to understand. He never forgot this scene. And according to both the prophecy of Jesus (21:18–19) and the most reliable tradition in the Christian church, he was eventually willing to lay down his life for Jesus.

If there was a vote in our churches on "Favorite Apostle," the winner would, quite possibly, be Simon Peter.

Why might that be so? Perhaps because of all the Apostles he is the one most obviously like us: a puzzle, and often a failure. And in addition, he was so often restored by his wonderful, gracious Savior—just as we need to be.

The senior minister under whom I first served once preached on this text: "Then the word of the LORD came to Jonah the second time" (Jonah 3:1). He gave the sermon the title "Failure Need Never Be Final." Those words have often echoed in my mind. I have shared Peter's immaturities, his misunderstanding, his lack of self-knowledge, and, yes, his failure in courage. You have too. But these failures need never be final if Peter's Savior is our Savior too.

Whenever we read to the end of John's gospel, we discover that this is the message it leaves with us. "The disciple whom Jesus loved" (John 21:20–24) tells us how Peter, who loved Christ, discovered that he was also "the disciple whom Jesus loved."

True, John's gospel describes only one disciple with these words. And they are usually understood to mean "loved more than the others." But what if they really mean he was "the disciple who discovered just how much Jesus loved him"?

If that is the case, then it is a discovery all of us can make.

5
—
Via, Veritas, Vita

John 14:1–14

"Let not your hearts be troubled. Believe in God; believe also in me. In my Father's house are many rooms. If it were not so, would I have told you that I go to prepare a place for you? And if I go and prepare a place for you, I will come again and will take you to myself, that where I am you may be also. And you know the way to where I am going." Thomas said to him, "Lord, we do not know where you are going. How can we know the way?" Jesus said to him, "I am the way, and the truth, and the life. No one comes to the Father except through me. If you had known me, you would have known my Father also. From now on you do know him and have seen him."

Philip said to him, "Lord, show us the Father, and it is enough for us." Jesus said to him, "Have I been with you so long, and you still do not know me, Philip? Whoever has seen me has seen the Father. How can you say, 'Show us the Father'? Do you not believe that I am in the Father and the Father is in me? The words that I say to you I do not speak on my own authority, but the Father who dwells in me does his works. Believe me that I am in the Father and the Father is in me, or else believe on account of the works themselves.

"Truly, truly, I say to you, whoever believes in me will also do the works that I do; and greater works than these will he do, because I am going to the Father. Whatever you ask in my name, this I will do, that the Father may be glorified in the Son. If you ask me anything in my name, I will do it."

What is the most frequently heard verse in John's gospel? John 3:16 may come immediately to mind: "For God so loved the world, that he gave his only Son . . ."

Or can words from the prologue (1:1–18) lay claim to this title? They are, after all, read every year at Christmastime.

But perhaps the most likely answer is John 14:1: "Let not your hearts be troubled . . ." They are read at almost every Christian funeral service.

This may help explain two things:

1. We rarely hear and reflect on these words in their original context. If you were to ask even regular churchgoers, "Tell me when Jesus said these words, and what happened before and after He said them," they might struggle to give an answer.

2. We tend to hear and read them as if they were spoken directly to us.

This is the way many—perhaps most—Christians always read the Bible. Of course, it is relevant to us today. But it is import-ant to remember that—like everything Jesus said in the upper room—while these words may apply to us, they were spoken only to the Apostles. We were not there. ⌐ !

Here, then, is a fundamental principle of Bible study: we reflect first on what the words communicated to those who heard them; then we work out, with the help of the Spirit, how they apply to us. ?

When we do that, we may find ourselves asking questions we might otherwise overlook and which in turn may help us pene-trate further into the meaning of the passage.

Here, for example, thinking about the original context of John 14:1 raises this question: How could Jesus say to His dis-ciples, "Don't let your hearts be troubled"? Doesn't that break a basic rule of counseling? After all, their problem was that they were troubled, and apparently for good reasons!

If troubled people could relieve themselves of their troubles, they would. Isn't telling them not to be troubled simply a counsel of despair? Did not Jesus know better than that?

But Jesus was a master counselor—so there must be something in the context here that helps us understand what He is doing.

In addition, if we read passages in their context, we are more likely to notice significant details. There is an important example here. John has just told us that "Jesus was troubled in his spirit" (13:21; the same verb is used in 14:1). A "troubled" Jesus is telling His disciples not to be "troubled"! Isn't this "the pot calling the kettle black"? A cynical reader might say, "Physician, heal your-self" (Luke 4:23).

Paradoxical? Yes, but this paradox provides a clue to help us understand Jesus' exhortation to His disciples. In fact, in its own way, it points us to the very heart of the gospel. Because Jesus was troubled, His disciples, both then and now, do not need to be! For what causes this trouble—His betrayal, arrest, shame, crucifixion, abandonment—is that He is bearing the burden of our deepest troubles: our guilt, our shame, and the death that is the wages of sin (Rom. 6:23). Since He knows and understands what it is like to be troubled, He can sympathize with us. Because He was troubled, in Him our troubled hearts can find peace.

The strength of Jesus' counsel lies in the way He explains why and how His disciples' hearts need not be troubled. For while there are reasons for their hearts to be troubled, there are greater reasons for not letting them be troubled. As the conversation unfolds, He will explain this further as He addresses the questions of two troubled disciples in particular.

What, then, is Jesus' counsel for the troubled heart? He is speaking here not about trivial upsets but about turmoil. He has been deeply agitated in spirit, and now His disciples are deeply agitated too. Their world is falling to pieces. They are feeling overwhelmed, and they have no control over the situation. How is it possible, under these circumstances, to have an untroubled heart? And is it possible, by way of application, for a Christian today to experience such heavenly poise?

Counsel for Troubled Hearts

What is the problem for the troubled heart? This: the circumstances that threaten us seem bigger and stronger than our resources to cope. We are like the disciples caught in the storm on the Sea of Galilee. Our skills and experience are not adequate for the situation.

Have you ever thought that Jesus was being a little unkind to His disciples when He asked them, "Why are you so afraid?" They surely had every reason to be—they were drowning! In fact, Jesus is gently diagnosing the problem. He asks: "Have you still no faith?" (Mark 4:40). In other words, there were resources available to them in the boat, Someone stronger than the winds and the waves, and they had ignored Him—or, to be more accurate, failed to trust Him.

You board an airplane. The bags are being loaded into the hold—23 kilos per bag for perhaps two hundred economy fares. Into the cabin come the passengers themselves, each weighing multiple kilos. You glance out of the window at the massive engines. Do you ever think, "How do planes ever get off the ground?" It is not because they are lighter than the air or because the law of gravity no longer exists. No, it is because the laws of aerodynamics are brought into operation: lift and thrust overcome weight and drag!

Something analogous is true for Christians. We are weighed down with trials and difficulties, perplexities, and deep sorrows. Being a Christian does not grant immunity from them. But there is another law at work. We have resources to overcome in Jesus Christ.

This is the point Paul makes: "we are more than conquerors" not because of our own strength but "through him who loved us" (Rom. 8:37).

Jesus' rebuke of the disciples did not imply, "Foolish disciples, you are seasoned fishermen and should have trusted your experience." No, it implied, "You had the Son of God in the boat, the Creator of Galilee and Ruler of the wind and the waves, but you did not trust Me." Their circumstances blinded them to the presence of their Savior. They were filled with fear rather than with faith.

Having Faith

We too often think of faith as passive—perhaps because we talk about "receiving" Christ. But there are active dimensions to faith. Our wise spiritual forefathers used to speak about "acting faith," that is, exercising faith, taking hold of God's promises, fixing our gaze on Christ and all He is (Heb. 3:1; 12:2).

Notice, then, the counsel Jesus gives to troubled hearts: "Believe, trust in God; trust also in Me."

Do not let your hearts be troubled. First, because God is your security: "The name of the LORD is a strong tower; the righteous man runs into it and is safe" (Prov. 18:10); "God is our refuge and strength, a very present help in trouble" (Ps. 46:1). No wonder Martin Luther used to say to his younger friend Philip Melanchthon whenever they were discouraged, "Come, Philip; let us sing the forty-sixth psalm!" No surprise, then, that his paraphrased application of it, "A Mighty Fortress Is Our God," became the anthem of the Reformation.

There is a logic implied in Jesus' words to the disciples: "Trust in God—therefore trust also in Me." God will be their refuge—they already know that; they have known Psalm 46 since they were children. But now they have been with Jesus for three years. They have every reason to trust Him, too, and to find their security in Him. They have seen the mighty works that have authenticated Him as the promised Messiah; they have heard Him speak of His unique relationship to His Father in heaven. Just as He came into the world to save them (John 3:16), He is leaving the world to prepare a place for them in His Father's presence: "In my Father's house are many rooms. If it were not so, would I have told you that I go to prepare a place for you? And if I go and prepare a place for you, I will come again and will take you to myself, that where I am you may be also" (14:2–3).

Follow the power of our Lord's logic here—for the strength of faith resides in grasping it:

Jesus' action: I am leaving you

Jesus' explanation: I am going to prepare a place for you in My Father's house

Jesus' conclusion: I am therefore going to return for you to take you home

See the logic? What theologians call Christology (who Jesus is and what He does) is the foundation for soteriology (how His work is savingly applied to our lives). It is worth underlining the point: the power of faith lies not in ourselves, or even in faith itself, but in Christ and the logic of the gospel. And even weak faith has this strong Christ as its object.

What patience and poise our Lord displays here in the context of overwhelming trouble. Such is His love for His disciples that He seems to be more concerned about their distress than He is about His own. This is the reason they—and we with them—can trust Him without reservation.

It may take time for this to sink in—that was certainly true for these disciples. But you can see the confidence it brings. No matter what happens, the biggest issue in life has been settled— our final destination in the Father's house. We are immortal until our work for the Lord Jesus is done. He has prepared a place for us. He is waiting for the day when He will bring us home to Himself.

We can hardly miss the implication—or can we? If these two things were true—His going to prepare a place for His disciples and His returning to take them there—then they could be sure He would keep them during the period in between. If that was true for them, then it is true for us too. If He has gone to heaven to prepare a place for us, and He is going to come from heaven to take us there, He will keep His hand on us during every in-between moment.

Perhaps Peter—frail and fallible Peter—was thinking of these very words when he later wrote:

Blessed be the God and Father of our Lord Jesus Christ! According to his great mercy, he has caused us to be born again to a living hope through the resurrection of Jesus Christ from the dead, to an inheritance that is imperishable, undefiled, and unfading, kept in heaven for you, who by God's power are being guarded through faith for a salvation ready to be revealed in the last time. In this you rejoice, though now for a little while, if necessary, you have been grieved by various trials, so that the tested genuineness of your faith—more precious than gold that perishes though it is tested by fire—may be found to

result in praise and glory and honor at the revelation of
Jesus Christ. (1 Peter 1:3–7)

All very well for Peter? After all, he had seen Jesus with his
own eyes and heard Him with his own ears. But notice what he
now adds: "Though you do not now see him, you believe in him
and rejoice with joy that is inexpressible and filled with glory,
obtaining the outcome of your faith, the salvation of your souls"
(vv. 8–9).

You believe in God? Believe also in Christ! Jesus gives the
disciples a further reason why their hearts need not be troubled:
"You know the way to where I am going" (John 14:4).

Knowing the Way

What was true for the Apostles is also true for His disciples in
every age. We know where He will take us, and we already know
the way there.

A young friend who used to come on summer mission with
our church's young people was standing in line one day in the
local butcher shop in his hometown. Two people were discuss-
ing whether it is possible to be sure you are going to heaven.
One of them denied it, but the other turned to my friend and
said, "Jimmy, you know that if you died tonight you would go
to heaven, don't you?" Jimmy replied quietly and happily, "Yes,
I do!"

The only reason I know this story is because I heard his minister tell it a few days later to a packed congregation—at Jimmy's
funeral service. An epileptic, he had died that night after a seizure
and gone to heaven.

But all this was not yet clear to at least two of the disciples in the upper room.

Answers for Troubled Disciples

Since Peter's outburst there had been further brief interchanges between him and Jesus. But now Thomas and Philip speak. Both are clearly still troubled.

Thomas

Thomas was puzzled—he was probably not alone in that. What did Jesus mean? His first recorded words to some of them were "Follow me." Perhaps the disciples thought then that they knew where He would lead them. But now they were not so sure. We can see ourselves in their shoes. The situation was overwhelming them; they were not capable of thinking clearly.

Perhaps Jesus was expecting a reaction when He said: "Since I am going to prepare a place for you, you can be absolutely sure that I will come back for you. In any event, you know the way to the place I am going. You know how to get there!" If so, He got one from Thomas. He was not so sure: "Thomas said to him, 'Lord, we do not know where you are going. How can we know the way?' "(John 14:5).

We often refer to this man as Doubting Thomas. Perhaps we are a little hard on him. But he was certainly Pessimistic Thomas. He seems to have been given to strong negative reactions. At least, he appears that way earlier in John's gospel. After Lazarus had died, Jesus decided to go to Bethany (a few miles away from Jerusalem, the epicenter of hostility to Him). Assuming the worst, Thomas responded, "Let us also go, that we may die with him" (11:16).

You probably know somebody who talks just like Thomas. It may even be you!

But at least Thomas is honest: "We don't know where You're going, so how can we know the way?"

If earlier Jesus had been saying, essentially, "Your hearts will be troubled until you start looking to Me," now He is saying, "Thomas, you're looking at the way but not seeing it": "I am the way, and the truth, and the life. No one comes to the Father except through me. If you had known me, you would have known my Father also. From now on you do know him and have seen him" (14:6–7).

What does He mean? What would "the way" have meant to these young Jewish disciples? The law of Moses was *halakhah*— the way. Unless they lapsed into formalism and legalism (which, alas, they often did), God's people knew that *torah* (law) was not merely a set of rules and regulations; it was a manual for a blessed life. That was why Moses had urged them to "choose life" (Deut. 30:19) and why the book of Psalms had opened with a poem describing the blessed life of the *torah*-guided man (Ps. 1:1–2).

Nevertheless, *torah* had been given to them in the form of written words. But now—as John had already explained in his prologue—the Word made flesh had come! So, Jesus is saying, "Thomas, don't you see that, now, I am *halakhah*?" He is the true *torah*, the true Word, and the true Way.

By saying that He is the truth, our Lord is not implying that the old covenant law and the lifestyle it promoted were false but saying that they were preliminary and temporary. The Mosaic law was given to God's people until the promised Messiah came.[1] Then, as Moses himself had recorded, God would raise up a new prophet, like Moses, but greater than he. The people were to listen to him (Deut. 18:18). He would be the truth.

Thomas was yet to understand this. But we have an advantage over him because John has been explaining it from the first page of his gospel. "The law was given through Moses; grace and truth came through Jesus Christ" (John 1:17). Moses was given only a "back view" of God. He did not see His face (Ex. 33:20); he only heard God speak about His grace (v. 19). But the Word of God, the Lord Jesus, is the One who was "face-to face with God." He is the "only Son from the Father, full of grace and truth." _Torah_ came through Moses, but "grace and truth" came to be "face-to-face" with us, John says, so that "we have seen his glory." Now the living Word has made the Father known to us (John 1:1–18).

John has been teaching us that Jesus is the reality to which the _torah_, the _halakhah_ of the old covenant, pointed forward. He is the Lamb of God (1:29); He turns the water used for the old covenant purification rites into wine (2:1–11); He is lifted up on the cross, just as Moses lifted up the serpent in the wilderness so that those who looked to it were saved (3:14); He is the true bread from heaven (6:32); He is the true Light of the World (8:12); He is the truly Good Shepherd (10:11).

The way to the Father is not to be found in the commandments and regulations per se but in the One to whom they all pointed, as a person's shadow sometimes appears before we see the person himself. While "the law was given through Moses; grace and truth came through Jesus Christ" (1:17).

The Old Testament law was given by the God of grace: "I am the LORD your God, who brought you out of the land of Egypt, out of the house of slavery" (Ex. 20:2). God graciously regulated sacrifices that covered over their sins. The law pointed to God's grace, but it was never intended to be identified with the grace to which it pointed. That came only in Jesus Christ. He is the true grace, grace in reality (1 Peter 5:12).

In a sense, Thomas is asking the question posed by the whole of the Old Testament: "Who shall ascend the hill of the LORD? And who shall stand in his holy place?" (Ps. 24:3). Now Jesus gives the answer: "Thomas, I am the true and life-giving *halakhah*. It is through faith in Me that you can come to the Father!"

It is still true. The law reveals the way to live. But at the same time, it reveals our sin (as Paul well understood; Rom. 7:7–13). But the Mosaic law as a whole gives us graphic symbolic pictures of the costliness of forgiveness. It points not to itself, but beyond itself—to Jesus Christ. John had earlier recorded the moment when John the Baptist had stood, as it were, on the shoulders of all the prophets of the old covenant period and pointed to Jesus: "Behold, the Lamb of God, who takes away the sin of the world!" (John 1:29). At last, the shadows were giving way to the reality.

Jesus now makes explicit what had been implicit: "No one comes to the Father except through me" (John 14:6).

The motto of my home city's late-medieval university was taken from the Latin Vulgate Bible's translation of John 14:6: *Via, Veritas, Vita*. Students in today's post–biblically literate society must wonder what it means. Is this the noble goal of a higher education—to find your "way" in "life" by seeking "truth" (if there is such) within these hallowed precincts? Perhaps ignorance of the words' origin protects them from being removed because, as a quotation from the Bible, they favor Christianity. Had the motto quoted the whole verse (which the founders would have assumed every student would instinctively complete), it surely would have been long since removed.[2] For the person quoted was saying that He, exclusively, is the way, the truth, and the life, and therefore the only way to God: "No one comes to the Father except through me."

You can almost hear the sneer of certain TV interviewers when you read these words. Skilled in the art of demeaning, they ask, "Are you really so arrogant that you believe that anyone who disagrees with you cannot go to heaven?" The implication being, "Shame, shame on you, you narrow-minded bigot!"

We should always be ready to give a reason for the hope that is in us (1 Peter 3:15). The question can be answered with integrity in more than one way.

The first—as should be obvious—is that we are not the person making the claim. The words are those of Jesus, recorded by "the Apostle of love"!

The second—equally obvious—is, What if this person is the Son of God who alone knows the Father (Matt. 11:27)? Has He no right to say that He alone can bring us to His Father?

The third—perhaps less obvious, but no less powerful—is this: If, in order to bring us into His presence, God the Father had to send His only Son to die on the cross—what possesses anyone to think they can devise another way? What miasma clouds my mind so that I cannot see that if God found no other way, then I certainly cannot? Has it never crossed my mind that a father will choose any way he can to protect his son from the kind of suffering associated with crucifixion—never mind an experience of God-forsakenness?

The arrogance lies elsewhere.

The issue is not, "Who do you think you are, Christian?"

It is, "Who do you think you are to believe you can accomplish on your own what God says could be accomplished only by the death of His Son on the cross?"

Imagine for a moment that you are standing before the judgment seat of God. The Father asks, "By what way do you expect to come into My heavenly presence?"

You reply, "Well, I found my own way here."

The Father responds, "But My own Son said that He was the only way, and that no one can come to Me except through Him."

You reply: "I knew He said that. But His words were too exclusive for my taste, so I have found my own way here."

The logic of our Lord's teaching here is that the conversation will end in this way:

The Father will say: "I sent My Son to be sacrificed on the cross. I laid the sins of the world on Him, and poured out the righteous wrath of heaven upon Him, and heard Him cry out, 'My God, My God, why have You forsaken Me?' Do you think I would have done that if there had been another way? My Son prayed, 'Father, if it is possible, let there be another way to bring them to heaven apart from the cross; please let this cup be taken from Me.' But I said to Him: 'My Son, there is no other way. Their only hope is if You drink this cup and bear the judgment against their sin. There is no other way.' Do you not think that if there had been another way, I certainly would have found it? Why have you despised My Son in this way?"

You say, "But I have arrived here by another way."

The Father will say: "Yes, you have arrived at the judgment seat of God. But you are on the way that leads to destruction."

We need to take with all seriousness Jesus' answer to Thomas' question, both for our own sake and for the sake of a lost world. There is no other way.

Philip

But now another disciple, of whom we read only occasionally in the Gospels, has a related but different request: "Philip said to him, 'Lord, show us the Father, and it is enough for us'" (John 14:8).

Is Jesus' response tinged with disappointment? "Have I been with you so long, and you still do not know me, Philip? Whoever has seen me has seen the Father" (v. 9).

Philip was a different personality from Thomas. He seems to have been the kind of person who tries to work things out on his own, and in the process sometimes forgets about Jesus!

Earlier in Jesus' ministry, a large crowd had followed Him from one side of the Sea of Galilee to the other. When He saw them coming, He asked: "Philip, where are we going to get food for this crowd?" (6:5).

Philip made a quick calculation—he reckoned there must be five thousand there—and that was only the men! "Jesus, a man's annual salary wouldn't buy enough to give each of them a couple of mouthfuls!"

Intriguingly, John tells us that Jesus already knew what He was going to do. He was testing Philip to see how he would respond to the problem (6:6; an approach every wise pastor occasionally employs!). Would he try to work out a plan of his own?

He tried, but there was nothing Philip could do. Andrew was more resourceful—perhaps he had greater faith, or was he simply a better "people person"? —he found a boy willing to share his lunch.

Philip had watched Jesus feed the multitude with a few fish and some bread rolls. Had he not already seen that the Father who had provided manna in the desert was revealing Himself in Jesus?

"Whoever has seen me has seen the Father. . . . Do you not believe that I am in the Father and the Father is in me?" (14:9).

Philip had tried to work out how to feed the multitude but had failed to take Jesus into account. He was making a similar mistake again. He had not understood that the answer to the bread problem was Jesus the Bread of Life (6:33). Now he fails to grasp that the answer to his seeing the Father problem is—once again—Jesus.

So, this time Jesus' reply expresses a deep sadness, as He said in essence:

> "After all this time with Me, Philip, you are still making the same mistake. You are still trying to solve the riddle without remembering that I am the key! After all these months in which I have shown you what the Father is like, and revealed Him to you, you should have understood. I have lived My whole life with you 'in' the Father—in fellowship with Him. Have you not heard My Father's voice in what I have said, and recognized My Father's presence and power in the works I have done? Philip, whoever has seen Me has seen the Father."

Recall again John's prologue: "No one has ever seen God; the only God, who is at the Father's side, he has made him known" (1:18). Jesus, the Word made flesh, was "at the Father's side [*eis ton kolpon*]"—we might say "right there with the Father, up close and personal." He was so intimately related to Him that He was able to make Him "known" (John uses the Greek verb *exēgeomai*, from which our word *exegesis* is derived).

To see Jesus is to see the Father. There is no confusion here of the two divine persons. The Father and Son are different in person and yet one in disposition. This is profoundly significant for our theology.

But these words are also profoundly significant at a personal level. They imply that there is nothing in the Father's character, or in His attitude toward us, that is different from what we find in Jesus. In this sense, to see Jesus is to see the Father. We need never fear there might be something hidden, perhaps even sinister, in Him.

Jesus had given Philip and the other disciples all the proof they needed to believe this. So He says to Philip: "Do you not believe that I am in the Father and the Father is in me? The words that I say to you I do not speak on my own authority, but the Father who dwells in me does his works" (14:10).

And then to them all: "Believe me that I am in the Father and the Father is in me, or else believe on account of the works themselves" (v. 11).

Jesus' works and words could only have come from "the Word . . . with God . . . the only God, who is at the Father's side." Did Philip not yet see that "He has made him known" (1:1, 18)?

Puzzling Words

This section closes with another of Jesus' "Truly, truly" sayings. But His words have often puzzled readers of John's gospel. That is perhaps not surprising when you consider what He said: "Truly, truly, I say to you, whoever believes in me will also do the works that I do; and greater works than these will he do, because I am going to the Father. Whatever you ask in my name, this I will do, that the Father may be glorified in the Son. If you ask me anything in my name, I will do it" (14:12–14).

Is this a blanket promise? If so, it raises all kinds of questions, not least this one: Should we be able to do the same works Jesus did—and even greater ones?

The answer is, surely, a simple no. After all, when Paul asked the question, "Do all work miracles? Do all possess gifts of healing?" (1 Cor. 12:29–30), he expected the answer no.[3]

Yes, we know that if we turn on the television to the appropriate channels, most days we will be able to see individuals who claim to be able to do that. They are ordinarily in large arenas, surrounded by their staff; their "greater works" tend to be of a limited kind; their theology is not usually the orthodoxy of the past two thousand years of the Christian church; and, sadly, their living standards are not often, if ever, characterized by the simplicity and modesty of the Lord Jesus, His Apostles, or, for that matter, the vast majority of ordinary Christian believers.

Given the ease with which we can be impressed by the spectacular, our Lord issued a sobering warning at the conclusion of His Sermon on the Mount: "Not everyone who says to me, 'Lord, Lord,' will enter the kingdom of heaven, but the one who does the will of my Father who is in heaven. On that day many [yes, many] will say to me, 'Lord, Lord, did we not prophesy in your name, and cast out demons in your name, and do many mighty works in your name?' And then I will declare to them, 'I never knew you; depart from me, you workers of lawlessness'" (Matt. 7:21–23).

So, casting out demons, and doing many mighty works—even

using Jesus' name—can, nevertheless, be the accomplishments of "workers of lawlessness."

But if Jesus' words here do not constitute a blanket promise to work miracles, or to heal as He did, how should we understand them? After all, He says "whoever believes in me" would do the works He did and even "greater works."

One view adopted by many interpreters is that Jesus is basically referring here to the fact that the Apostles will see many more people coming to faith in Christ than he did himself.

But a closer examination of the text may suggest a different interpretation.

We have already underlined that in reading these chapters it is important to remember: Jesus was not addressing us; we were not there. We cannot therefore assume that everything our Lord said applies to us in the same way it applied to the Apostles.

With this in mind, notice the transitions in Jesus' words: "I say to *you*, [1] whoever believes in me . . . [he] will also do the works that I do' " (v. 12); "[I say to *you* . . .] [2] Whatever *you* ask in my name . . . If *you* ask me anything . . ." (vv. 13–14).[4]

Jesus appears to be underlining that His words are addressed specifically to the Apostles. They are the "you" of verse 13. Perhaps therefore we should understand the "whoever" and the "he" and the "you" in verse 12 as referring to them too. If so, the whole section from verse 12 through verse 14 is a promise made to the men who were in the room listening to Him, to the Apostles. So, the principle that helps us is this: when Jesus spoke these words, the only people who heard them were the eleven remaining Apostles. He is saying specifically to them: "Let Me emphasize to you, My dear troubled Apostles, whoever of you trusts Me the way I have just been urging you . . . will do even greater works than you have seen Me do. . . . In fact, whatever you ask . . . anything . . . I will do it!"

Remember what we have already noted: we should not assume that everything Jesus said is spoken to us as if we were there with Him. We were not there; nor are we Apostles.[5]

We instinctively understand that some of Jesus' statements were made to specific individuals, not to everyone. One obvious example is His command to the rich young ruler to sell everything he owned, distribute the proceeds to the poor, and follow Him (Luke 18:22).

Again, Jesus told the disciples to wait in Jerusalem to receive the Holy Spirit (Luke 24:49).

We recognize that there may be applications of these statements that are relevant to us. But we do not misunderstand Jesus to be saying that every Christian must impoverish himself in order to be a disciple, or that we should spend several weeks in Jerusalem waiting to receive the Holy Spirit.

So, again, the principle that helps us here is that the only people who heard Jesus speak these words were the eleven remaining Apostles. So, His words "Whoever believes in me . . ." are not addressed to all and sundry but specifically to the men He had urged earlier to believe in Him (John 14:1).

This interpretation is further confirmed if we recognize that these words are not so much a general promise but a specific prophecy that had its fulfillment in the lives of the Apostles. They did in fact do the works Jesus did. And indeed, as He promised, they did "even greater works."

The Acts of the Apostles describes how they healed many (3:7,

16; 5:14–16; 8:6–7; 9:34–41; 14:8–10; 19:9–12; 28:8–9). More than that, it tells us of the large numbers of people who came to faith compared to the relatively small numbers who did so during Jesus' own ministry. He never saw three thousand people press into the kingdom after a single sermon or the increase in numbers that Luke records in the first days of the young church (2:41, 47; 4:4; 5:14; 6:7; 9:31; 11:21, 24; 12:24). So, Jesus' promise-prophecy came true. It is also clear from the book of Acts that all this was in answer to prayer (1:4; 2:42; 4:24–31). They prayed in Christ's name, according to His will, and it was done for them![6]

It is clear now how Jesus' promise-prophecy fits into this whole section of His teaching. It opened with troubled disciples. Now they have been given specific promises to encourage them.

There had been no time since the crisis on the Sea of Galilee when these men had faced a situation as overwhelming as the one they were now experiencing. All they have lived for, all the sacrifices they had made, and all their hopes, were crumbling around them: their Master was leaving them! His promise to return sometime in the unknown future was no compensation for the prospect of His impending absence. What were they to do? There was no one else to whom they could turn.

Here is Jesus' answer. Not only must they resist being overwhelmed by their troubled hearts tonight; they must be reassured that they will see the great works of God in the future. The Lord's presence will continue with them—in a new and wonderful way. The Lord's work will continue—in an even greater way. "Having loved his own who were in the world," Jesus was going to love them "to the end" (John 13:1).

Unbelievable? Perhaps it seemed so. But that is why Jesus

opened and closed this section of His teaching by urging them to trust in Him (John 14:1, 12). If they did—and they did—they would see Him do wonderful things through them.

Here is something endlessly amazing. Our Lord is destined to experience so much suffering, pain, and humiliation; He will be betrayed, denied, abandoned, shamed, beaten, and crucified; He knows that in an hour or so He will be prostrate before His Father in the garden of Gethsemane asking if there is any other way. Yet under this crushing burden, He speaks these words to comfort and encourage His disciples.

But it is just as amazing for us to know that "Jesus Christ is the same yesterday and today and forever" (Heb. 13:8).

What scripture can we apply to today?
Paul's letters were to the Ephesians
How can they apply to us?
When is healing genuine?
Why pray?

verses

Originates, implements, enfills

Ephesians 1

Saved - sealed with Holy Spirit

Isaiah Spirit of the Lord -

Present but not indwelling

Romans 8 - the Spirit that raised Jesus is in me

Encouraging

Same Spirit will raise me

Brothers with Christ

Ezekiel - new spirit

Gifts of Spirit

6

—

Threefold Spirit

John 14:15–31

"If you love me, you will keep my commandments. And I will ask the Father, and he will give you another Helper, to be with you forever, even the Spirit of truth, whom the world cannot receive, because it neither sees him nor knows him. You know him, for he dwells with you and will be in you.

"I will not leave you as orphans; I will come to you. Yet a little while and the world will see me no more, but you will see me. Because I live, you also will live. In that day you will know that I am in my Father, and you in me, and I in you. Whoever has my commandments and keeps them, he it is who loves me. And he who loves me will be loved by my Father, and I will love him and manifest myself to him." Judas (not Iscariot) said to him, "Lord, how is it that you will manifest yourself to us, and not to the world?" Jesus answered him, "If anyone loves me, he will keep my word, and my Father will love him, and we will come to him and make our home with him. Whoever does not love me does not keep my words. And the word that you hear is not mine but the Father's who sent me.

"These things I have spoken to you while I am still with you. But the Helper, the Holy Spirit, whom the Father will send in my name, he will teach you all things and bring to your remembrance all that I have said to you. Peace I leave with you; my peace I give to you. Not as the world gives do I give to you. Let not your hearts be troubled, neither let them be afraid. You heard me say to you, 'I am going away, and I will come to you.' If you loved me, you would have rejoiced, because I am going to the Father, for the Father is greater than I. And now I have told you before it takes place, so that when it does take place you may believe. I will no longer talk much with you, for the ruler of this world is coming. He has no claim on me, but I do as the Father has commanded me, so that the world may know that I love the Father. Rise, let us go from here."

O ne of the most famous works to emerge from the Protestant Reformation was less like a book and more like a transcription of podcasts. Everyone refers to it simply as *Table Talk*—and the "talker"? Martin Luther.

The life of a seminary professor in the sixteenth century differed in many respects from today. Professor Luther and his wife, Katie, "took in" students, perhaps a dozen at a time. At mealtimes, a relaxed Luther—but still ever the teacher—would express his views freely (a little too freely at times!) on a seemingly end-less supply of topics. His students, as students do, found ways of recording his comments for posterity.

John 13–17 is Jesus' table talk to His eleven faithful disciples on the evening of His passion. What He said was permanently lodged in John's memory. At this stage in John's account of the evening, Jesus has just said that He is the way—indeed, the only way—to the Father. He had reassured the disciples that He was going to the Father to prepare a place for them. They should therefore not allow their hearts to be overwhelmed by their present circumstances.

Despite this, the disciples' mood is somber: their Master is about to leave them.

Later, Jesus will tell them directly that His leaving them is to their "advantage." And He will explain why. Unless He leaves them, "the Helper will not come to you" (16:7).

These later words probably struck Jesus' disciples as cold comfort. It was inconceivable to them that there could be any adequate compensation for His leaving them, never mind an "advantage." They would need an entire paradigm shift in their thinking to be able to take that in. Even after He has told them, they will still have things to learn that they cannot now "bear" (16:12). But the truth is they could scarcely bear what Jesus was telling them now, never mind what they would learn in the future.

Paradigm Shift

Knowing this, our Lord shows the patience and wisdom that are hallmarks of His ministry as His disciples' Teacher. Here, before He tells them directly that His leaving will be to their "advantage," He prepares the way by talking to them about the coming of the Spirit.

The Scots have a saying: "Some things are better felt than telt" (we only begin to appreciate some things when we experience them ourselves). Otherwise, we are describing scenes to people without sight, or aromas to people with no sense of smell.

So, here in John 14:15–31, Jesus is laying the groundwork for what He will later tell His disciples. He is going to leave them. He needs to leave them for their own sake; otherwise, the Helper, the Holy Spirit, will not come to them. If He leaves, He will send Him to them.

Do you think the Master's using the word "advantage" would have set their minds at rest? Hardly. All the disciples would "hear" would be the word "leave." Nothing could compensate for His absence. In their eyes, the presence of the Helper would be poor and inadequate compensation for the absence of Jesus. They do not, indeed they cannot, understand that the Spirit will come to them as the Spirit of Jesus. They cannot yet grasp what it means that they will be indwelt by one and the same Spirit who was present with their Lord throughout the thirty-three years of His ministry. Instead of losing Him, they will gain Him in a new and more intimate way! But until they understand who the Spirit is, the idea that Jesus' departure could be in any way advantageous to them would remain utterly inconceivable.

We can appreciate how they must have felt. After all—Which would you rather have?

1. Jesus with you in the flesh, so that you could hear His voice, see His face, tell the color of His eyes, watch His gesticulations and His facial mannerisms—everything about Him.

Or:

2. The Holy Spirit with you.

Wouldn't you choose Jesus?

If so, you can understand how impossible it was for the Apostles to think of Jesus' departure and the Spirit's coming as an "advantage." They were incapable of that kind of calculation. So, what Jesus now teaches them is intended to prepare the ground for the new paradigm that will restructure their thinking.

√ Helper

Jesus promises the Apostles that they will receive help: "I will ask the Father, and he will give you another Helper, to be with you forever, even the Spirit of truth, whom the world cannot receive, because it neither sees him nor knows him. You know him, for he dwells with you and will be in you" (John 14:16–17).

The words "another Helper" translate the Greek *allos paraklētos*. The root meaning of *paraklētos* is "someone called [*klētos*] alongside [*para*]" to help, encourage, and counsel.

In English, the word "another" can have two different nuances: (1) "another of the same kind" (as in, "That was a delicious chocolate chip cookie; may I have another?") and (2) "another of a different kind" (as in, "I am allergic to the nuts in these cookies; do you have another one—perhaps a plain one?").

In Greek, however, there are two different words for "another": *allos* (= another of the same kind) and *heteros* (= another of a different kind, as in Galatians 1:6).

In all languages, over time words can lose their distinctive nuances and be used in looser ways than their dictionary definitions (and sometimes even develop new meanings). That seems to have been true of *allos* and *heteros*. But here, clearly, the formal distinction is maintained. When Jesus says He is going to send *allos paraklētos*, He means "another Helper of the same kind as the Helper you have already known and experienced." That original Helper was Jesus Himself. He is saying: "I am going to send a Helper of the same kind as I have been."

But then He adds something remarkable: this "other" Paraclete will not only be with them (as Jesus has been); He will dwell in them and be with them forever!

As readers of John's gospel, we know more about what will happen than the disciples did at this stage. We know from the rest of the New Testament that they are not going to lose Jesus' presence but gain it in a new and more intimate way. For the coming of the Helper will be not only like Jesus' living with them but having Him living in them—forever!

Our Lord spells this out for them. As they continue to walk in loving obedience to Him, God's purposes will unfold. They fear they will be orphaned. But the reverse will be the case, for now they will taste the love of both the Father and the Son (14:21, 23). Rather than being deprived of the ministry that Jesus has exercised among them, they will experience that ministry forever. If they only realized what was happening, they would have been rejoicing rather than fearing (vv. 27–28).

Who then is this *allos paraklētos* who comes as the Helper of the disciples?

Woven into John 14:15–31 are three pictures of His ministry.

Counselor

The Spirit will come as their Helper in the sense that He would be their Counselor, someone they could call on to encourage them and give them counsel.

Throughout His ministry, Jesus had been the disciples' Counselor. He was still counseling them in the upper room. He had counseled them not to be troubled; He had answered their questions, leading them gently from misunderstanding to understanding. Now He promises that the Spirit will assume and continue that role in their lives.

But the word *paraklētos* has undertones that may not be immediately obvious to us. It is used five times in the New Testament, only by John, and (with one exception) only in these chapters in John's gospel where it refers to the Holy Spirit (14:16, 26; 15:26; 16:7).

The one exception is significant because it helps us catch a special nuance in John's use of the word. He writes in his first letter: "But if anyone does sin, we have [a *paraklētos*] with the Father, Jesus Christ the righteous" (1 John 2:1).[1]

The Christian has two Paracletes—the Spirit of God dwelling within him and the Son of God at the right hand of the Father! Paul uses different language to say the same thing: the indwelling Spirit makes intercession for the saints, and the Lord Jesus also intercedes for them at the right hand of God (Rom. 8:26, 34).

Almost without exception, English versions of the Bible translate *paraklētos* in 1 John 2:1 as "advocate." That word has a legal undertone—the *paraklētos* is our Helper, Encourager, Comforter, and Counselor because He serves as our advocate.

Think of the words you may have seen on a letterhead from a law office: "counselor-at-law." It is a traditional way of describing a lawyer—someone who is qualified to act on your behalf in matters related to the law, to be your advocate—and if necessary, to plead your case in court and serve as your defense counsel.

Jesus had fulfilled the role of *paraklētos* for the disciples. He had "taken their case" throughout His earthly ministry. He will not forget His brief when He goes to the right hand of God. But He knows His disciples will still require an Advocate on earth; they will need encouragement and wise counsel; they will need to know how to live faithful Christian lives. Who will give this when Jesus leaves? Jesus reassures them that the Spirit will continue the ministry He began.

There is, however, an important difference between the world of the counselor-at-law today and his or her counterpart in the world to which Jesus belonged.

If someone needs legal counsel today, he goes downtown to an office with a sign outside, often with two, three, or more names on it. You already know that even the most junior lawyers have been taught how to bill by hourly or even five-minute intervals, so you are expecting a significant financial commitment! The law is a profession: the rules, the standards, and the scale of fees are all set out somewhere in writing.

When we read the references to "lawyers" in the Gospels, we might mistake them for first-century equivalents. But "lawyer" in the Gospels really means "law-scholar," not "advocate in court." That is why the lawyers mentioned in the Gospels liked to discuss the meaning of the laws of Moses and to ask Jesus questions of interpretation, such as: "If I am to love my neighbor, what is the definition of 'neighbor'?" Or "which is the greatest commandment?"

Lawyers were, therefore, interpreters of the law, not men who defended you when you were in trouble. A lawyer was not a *parakletos*. If you needed somebody to speak up for you before the judges, a *parakletos*, you asked a close friend, whose testimony could be trusted because he knew you intimately. You might ask your longest-standing friend: "Will you help me and be my paraclete; will you serve as my counselor? I am in trouble, and I need you to speak for me and defend me." Such a friend could speak up on your behalf in court and say: "Let me tell you the truth. My friend is innocent. Nobody knows him as well as I do. I have known him all his life. You can trust me; believe me!"

This is exactly the case with "the Spirit of truth" (John 14:17), first in relationship to Jesus and then to His disciples. He was, truly, Jesus' longest-standing and closest "friend."

Think about it. The Spirit was actively present when the Lord Jesus was conceived in the womb of the Virgin Mary (Matt. 1:20; Luke 1:35). He enabled Jesus to grow in wisdom and in favor with God during His early years (Luke 2:52; see Isa. 11:2–3). He was present at His baptism and temptations (Luke 3:22; 4:1). He empowered Him throughout His ministry (Luke 4:14, 18) and as He cast out demons (Matt. 12:28). He was the One through whom Jesus offered Himself up to the Father (Heb. 9:14) and by whose power He was raised from the dead (Rom. 1:4). He accompanied Him from the womb to the tomb.

The Spirit was Jesus' Counselor. He bore witness to Him. He was with Him through every step of His life; He knew Him best. We might indeed say that He was our Lord's "Best Friend."

This is why the Holy Spirit's ministry to us is so significant. He knows Jesus best, and He knows us best too. He knows how to teach us about Jesus and what resources to bring to us from Jesus. He is like a bright light shining now on this aspect, now on that aspect of Jesus' character and ministry, showing us that He is exactly the Savior we need.

What an advantage! "I am going from you," Jesus says, "but I will send another Counselor to you, the Spirit of truth." And because He is the Spirit of truth, we can rely on Him absolutely.

It is because of this that we want to love and honor Jesus. Picture the counselor-at-law turning to his client and giving him advice. The Spirit's advice to us is: "Keep your eyes fixed on Christ. See how wonderful He is. Trust Him. Live for Him. Don't let Him down. Follow Him. Serve Him all your life." And because of His ministry, we respond: "Yes, I want to do that. Empower me to do it!" And so, through His ongoing counsel, we keep looking to Christ and loving and serving Him.

But there is another word-picture Jesus uses here to describe the Spirit's ministry. It may be less familiar and expressed in less theological terminology, but it is no less significant.

Homemaker

Jesus had been the disciples' Counselor. Now that role would be continued by the Spirit. But earlier in the evening, as John remembered, Jesus had also described Himself as a Homemaker for the disciples.

If a wife and mother who is not employed outside the home fills in a form that has a line for "Occupation," she writes "Homemaker." It is a much happier description than the now old-fashioned "Housewife." That described a location ("house") and a relationship ("wife"). But it did not in itself describe what a person did, her occupation. "Homemaker" does. It describes someone who, in a hundred different ways, is occupied as the person who transforms a house into a home and the person who creates the family atmosphere.

Now, think of a situation—after a church service, for example—when a mother says to the rest of the family, "We have guests coming; I will go home just now, before the rest of you, to get everything ready for them."

That is the role Jesus tells the disciples He will fulfill for them! He is their Homemaker: "In my Father's house are many rooms. If it were not so, would I have told you that I go to prepare a place for you?" (John 14:2).

The disciples believe that Jesus is leaving far too early! But Jesus teaches them the reason for His departure: He is going to be their Homemaker in heaven.

We can well understand if the disciples thought that this was all very well for the there-and-then; but what about the here-and-now? But Jesus gives them good news: the Spirit will come to be their Homemaker here and now to get them ready for there and then!

See what this means for them—and for us: "I will not leave you as orphans; I will come to you" (14:18). Since their Homemaker was leaving, they inevitably felt that they were being orphaned. But no, the Spirit would come. How, then, would His coming relieve them of this terrible sense of being orphaned? Because, despite all their faults, they genuinely loved Jesus, and the coming of the Spirit would realize His promise to them: "If anyone loves me, he will keep my word, and my Father will love him, and we [that is, the Father and the Son][2] will come to him and make our home with him"(14:23).

Here is one of Scripture's most moving pictures of the Spirit's ministry. Jesus will send Him to them so that they will become men in whose lives the Father and the Son will feel at home!

It is a simple domestic picture. "There is nowhere like home," we say. But sometimes we find ourselves in homes where a cold or awkward atmosphere prevails, and we do not feel really welcome. We are relieved when it is time to leave. Other homes are suffused with an atmosphere of love, and their open-hearted welcome embraces us. It says, "Make yourself at home." And we do. We are so much at home that we scarcely notice the passage of time.

This is what the Spirit's ministry is like. He not only enables us to feel at home with God (we will not feel orphaned) but transforms us so that we become men and women about whom the Father might say to the Son, "I feel at home there, don't You?"

But there is also a challenge implied here. This does not happen automatically, as Jesus explains when He answers Judas' question about why He would show Himself to the disciples but not to the world.[3] He comes to, and He and the Father make Their home with, only those who trust, love, and obey Him (14:21, 23).

Is that you?

This picture of the Spirit's ministry as "homemaker" suggests two further reflections.

First, it helps explain why the Christian life is full of challenges. After all, the Spirit is transforming us into a home fit for the Father and Son to live in comfortably! There is major reconstruction to be done and regular spring cleaning. As C.S. Lewis graphically expressed it:

> Imagine yourself as a living house. God comes in to rebuild that house. At first, perhaps, you can understand what He is doing. He is getting the drains right and stopping the leaks in the roof and so on: you knew that those jobs needed doing and so you are not surprised. But presently He starts knocking the house about in a way that hurts abominably and does not seem to make sense. What on earth is He up to? The explanation is that He is building quite a different house from the one you thought of—throwing out a new wing here, putting on an extra floor there, running up towers, making courtyards. You thought you were going to be made into a decent little cottage: but He is building a palace. He intends to come and live in it Himself.[4]

But, second, there is an appropriateness in thinking about the Holy Spirit as Homemaker.

In the Western world, if a woman who is not employed outside the family home answers the question "What do you do?" by saying, "I am a homemaker," she may sometimes feel demeaned by the response she receives, such as "Oh, so you don't do anything" or "You don't do anything else." The implication is often this: you are not worth much if that is all you do.

Three cheers, then, for Jesus, for using this picture to describe His "Best Friend"! Like a homemaker, the Spirit does not draw attention to Himself. His passion is not to glorify Himself but Jesus (16:14) and to transform lives for the Father and the Son to indwell with comfort. In every loving family, the homemaker is well known and much loved, even adored—because she is the one on whom the happiness of the home depends. True, the Spirit glorifies not Himself but Jesus. But that is another reason to honor Him for His ministry. No wonder the church fathers who composed the Nicene Creed in AD 325 confessed that "with the Father and the Son he is to be worshiped and glorified"!

So, the ministry of Christ as Advocate and Homemaker would be continued by the Spirit. And, significantly, so would a third dimension of the Master's work.

Teacher

Jesus Himself had been the disciples' Teacher. Even in the upper room, He had been teaching them. He had patiently answered their questions, helping them understand what He said. They called him Teacher, and He accepted that description (John 13:13).

Now, however, they are losing their teacher. But once again, Jesus reassures them that they will continue to be taught—because they still have much to learn (13:7; 16:12). When the Paraclete comes, He will also be their Teacher: "These things I have spoken to you while I am still with you. But the Helper, the Holy Spirit, whom the Father will send in my name, he will teach you all things and bring to your remembrance all that I have said to you" (14:25–26).

But how?

John himself experienced the fulfillment of this promise. His gospel is the result. Not only does it record what was brought to his "remembrance" of what Jesus "said," but it also includes some of the "all things" the Spirit taught him to see and understand about his Master.

What, then, will the disciples learn?

Paul tells us that the Spirit of God searches "the depths of God" and makes them known to us (1 Cor. 2:10–13). There is nothing about God the eternal Trinity or about the ministry of the Lord Jesus that is hidden from the Spirit. So, says Jesus, when the Holy Spirit comes, "in that day [i.e., Pentecost] you will know that I am in my Father . . ." (John 14:20).

In other words, when the Holy Spirit comes, the disciples will have an even deeper understanding of Jesus' relationship to His Father and of the intimacy of their fellowship: "In that day you will know that I am in my Father."

What does the preposition "in" mean?

When Augustine was asked about the meaning of "time," he replied that he thought he knew until he was asked the question![5] Prepositions can be like that. We use the preposition *in* all the time. So, we know perfectly well what it means. But if someone asks us, "What does Jesus mean when He says that the Son is 'in' the Father?" we realize that the preposition takes us out of our depth.

Many years later, perhaps remembering that at the table that night he had been "at Jesus' side [*en tō kolpō*]" (13:23), John penned the first words of his gospel: "The Word was with God [*pros ton theon*—toward God, face-to-face] . . . at the Father's side [*eis ton kolpon*] . . ." (1:1, 18). Did he see in his own experience of fellowship with Jesus, in knowing he was the disciple "whom Jesus loved," a reflection of Jesus' own relationship to His Father as "the Son the Father loved"?

Throughout the gospel, John mentions the ways he had seen this: the glory of the Son in His relationship to the Father; the ways the Father had shown His love for the Son, and the Son had reciprocated that love (3:35; 10:17). The disciples' eyes had not yet been opened to all this; but Jesus was giving them hints of the privileges that awaited them when the Spirit came.

But if the Spirit will teach them deep things about Jesus' relationship to the Father, He will also teach them deep things about His relationship to them: "In that day," Jesus says, "you will know that I am in my Father, and you in me, and I in you." There is a parallel between the relationship our Lord has with His Father and the relationship the disciples will have with Him. This, too, they will experience when the Paraclete comes.

It is as if Jesus is saying: "Throughout My ministry, I was with you, but always outside of you. You see Me. You can touch Me. You hear Me. But when the Holy Spirit comes as One like Me, He who indwells Me will indwell you. He will live in you and transform and empower you from within."

So long as Jesus is physically present with them, He cannot also dwell in them. He must leave them if He is to dwell in them.

This is an amazing promise. The disciples fear that if Jesus leaves them, their relationship with Him will come to an end. But the reverse is the case. When He leaves and the Spirit comes, they will mutually indwell each other.

The Spirit-given union between the Lord Jesus and His people is one of the great mysteries of the gospel. But it lies at the heart of the Christian life, as Paul points out:

> You, however, are not in the flesh but in the Spirit, if in
> fact the Spirit of God dwells in you. Anyone who does
> not have the Spirit of Christ does not belong to him. But

if Christ is in you, although the body is dead because of sin, the Spirit is life because of righteousness. If the Spirit of him who raised Jesus from the dead dwells in you, he who raised Christ Jesus from the dead will also give life to your mortal bodies through his Spirit who dwells in you. (Rom. 8:9–11)

To be indwelt by the Spirit is to have Christ Himself dwelling in us and to experience what Paul describes as "Christ in you, the hope of glory" (Col. 1:27).

This helps explain Jesus' enigmatic statement about the Spirit: "You know him, for he dwells with you and will be in you" (John 14:17).

Prepositions

The Spirit "dwells with you and will be in you." Jesus' words are often interpreted as His way of describing the difference between believers in the old and new covenant dispensations: the Spirit was (only) *with* believers in the old covenant period, whereas now in the new covenant He is *in* them.

This, however, seems inadequate. It suggests that the Spirit's work under the old covenant was only external. It is true that the Spirit does work externally to fulfill God's purposes, and also that He is the source of all good gifts. But the Apostolic writings teach us that the fruit produced by the Spirit's indwelling believers under the new covenant was already present in the lives of believers under the old covenant. Think how often the New Testament illustrates gospel grace and its fruit by appealing to individuals who lived under the old covenant. It would be strange indeed if what is effected in the new only by the Spirit's being "in" believers was perfectly capable of being effected in the old by His merely being "with" them. Yes, there is a fullness to the Spirit's ministry when He comes as the Spirit of Christ, but there is, surely, continuity in the way that He relates to believers.

What, then, did Jesus mean? It is more likely that He meant something like this: "You already know the Helper, the Spirit of truth, because He has been present with you, indwelling Me. But when I send Him from the Father, He—the very same Spirit—is going to be present indwelling you. Yes, the same Spirit who these thirty-three years has been present in My life—with all the resources of His presence in My life, holiness, and love—will indwell you."

One and the same Spirit—the identical Spirit—who anointed Jesus indwells all Christians!

Think of it this way: The Holy Spirit indwells Jesus; and now the Holy Spirit indwells His disciples. How many Holy Spirits are there? Two? The Spirit who indwells Jesus and the Spirit who indwells believers?

No, only one.

Or ask the question a different way: Since the Holy Spirit indwells every individual Christian, how many Holy Spirits are there? Hundreds, thousands, millions? A Holy Spirit for each believer?

No, only one.

There is only one Holy Spirit, one Paraclete. All Christians are indwelt by one and the same Spirit—and He is one and the same Spirit who was present in the incarnate life of the Son of God.

We can articulate this theology easily enough. But who can grasp its implications? If there is only one Spirit, then the Spirit the Lord Jesus promised to send to the disciples must be the very same Spirit who indwelt Him. The Spirit Jesus sent to the church after His ascension is the Spirit who for thirty-three years was present in His life. If He indwells us, no deeper intimacy of fellowship with Jesus is possible. And no deeper fellowship with others is possible either. We share one Spirit not only with Christ but with one another!

This is the promise Jesus is giving His disciples. They are "losing" their Teacher only to "gain" Him in a new way.

Later, we will see more about how the Spirit is our Teacher. But for the moment we should note that if He indwells us, He is able to do what all teachers wish they could do for their pupils—get inside them and teach them not only from the outside, by providing "revelation," but from the inside, by giving "illumination." The Paraclete-Teacher sent by Jesus will do precisely this. He is the giver of the revelation of the New Testament and the provider of illumination. He thus enables us to understand the revelation and warms our hearts to receive it. In this sense, the Spirit continues the ministry Jesus exercised on the road to Emmaus: He illumines our understanding and "strangely warms" our hearts (see Luke 24:13–35). In this way, Jesus Himself will come to the obedient disciples and manifest Himself to them (John 14:21).

The Next Stage

As Jesus brings this section of His teaching to a close, He says to the disciples, "Let us go from here" (John 14:31). Many scholars have held that they must have left the room at this point and perhaps made their way from the upper room to the garden of Gethsemane via the temple. But John gives no indication of this, and he suggests that it was only later that they did so (in 18:1). The words therefore seem a little puzzling.

It may be that the conversation simply continued, as sometimes happens when we have said we are about to leave! But there is another possibility. Jesus has just been talking about the impending attack of the devil. He says, "The ruler of this world is coming." But while Satan may be "ruler of this world," he has no authority over the Lord Jesus: "He has no claim on me, but I do as the Father has commanded me, so that the world may know that I love the Father. Rise, let us go [*agōmen*] from here" (14:30–31).

The verb John uses here (*agōmen*) was sometimes employed in a military context of troops advancing to meet the enemy ("Up and at them!"). If this is in John's mind, then Jesus is not talking about their immediate physical departure but about His impending conflict; the movement is not geographical but spiritual: "Since the enemy is coming, let us go to meet him."

John knew that "the whole world lies in the power of the evil one" (1 John 5:19). The disciples are about to go into the "night" where he reigns. But Jesus is Lord in the darkness of the Jerusalem night as well as in the light of the upper room. And although there will be dark days in the future for the disciples, He has promised to send them "another Helper" who will be with them forever. The last battle has begun, but they will be kept safe.

7

—

The True Vine

John 15:1–17

"I am the true vine, and my Father is the vinedresser. Every branch in me that does not bear fruit he takes away, and every branch that does bear fruit he prunes, that it may bear more fruit. Already you are clean because of the word that I have spoken to you. Abide in me, and I in you. As the branch cannot bear fruit by itself, unless it abides in the vine, neither can you, unless you abide in me. I am the vine; you are the branches. Whoever abides in me and I in him, he it is that bears much fruit, for apart from me you can do nothing. If anyone does not abide in me he is thrown away like a branch and withers; and the branches are gathered, thrown into the fire, and burned. If you abide in me, and my words abide in you, ask whatever you wish, and it will be done for you. By this my Father is glorified, that you bear much fruit and so prove to be my disciples. As the Father has loved me, so have I loved you. Abide in my love. If you keep my commandments, you will abide in my love, just as I have kept my Father's commandments and abide in his love. These things I have spoken to you, that my joy may be in you, and that your joy may be full.

"This is my commandment, that you love one another as I have loved you. Greater love has no one than this, that someone lay down his life for his friends. You are my friends if you do what I command you. No longer do I call you servants, for the servant does not know what his master is doing; but I have called you friends, for all that I have heard from my Father I have made known to you. You did not choose me, but I chose you and appointed you that you should go and bear fruit and that your fruit should abide, so that whatever you ask the Father in my name, he may give it to you. These things I command you, so that you will love one another."

The Vine and the branches. This is a familiar and much-loved passage. Whole books have been written on it. Sometimes entire theologies of the Christian life have been built on its themes—especially the idea of "abiding in Christ."

Jesus had already spoken about the new relationship His disciples would have with Him through the indwelling of the Spirit: "You in me, and I in you" (John 14:20). Now He describes it by means of an extended metaphor they could all understand: He is the Vine, they are the branches. His Father is the Vinedresser, whose goal is that they will "bear much fruit." In order for that to happen, two things are essential: their vital union with Christ and their pruning by the Father.

Perhaps a good way to highlight the emphasis in Jesus' teaching from John 14:15 onward is by asking this question: What is the New Testament's most common way of describing Christians? Strangely enough, it is not as a "Christian." If you skim through the pages of the New Testament, it will soon strike you that the word "Christian" rarely appears—only three times, to be exact:

> Acts 11:26: "And in Antioch the disciples were first called Christians."

> Acts 26:28: "And Agrippa said to Paul, 'In a short time would you persuade me to be a Christian?' "

> 1 Peter 4:16: "Yet if anyone suffers as a Christian, let him not be ashamed, but let him glorify God in that name."

In at least two (and possibly all three) of these instances, "Christian" seems to be a term of abuse, perhaps with the kind of connotation the word Puritan had in the seventeenth century, or *fundamentalist* often has today. Those who trusted in Christ were called "Christians"—Christ's ones. They themselves seem to have preferred other terms such as "saints," "disciples," or "believers."

Yet none of these terms is the most common New Testament description. That honor belongs to the expression "in Christ." It (and its equivalents such as "in Him") occurs around two hundred times.

This—our union with Christ—is the heartbeat of the Christian life, and here, in John 15, Jesus is helping His disciples to understand what it means. He had already begun to do this by explaining that when His Spirit came to indwell them, they would experience an even more intimate relationship with Him: they would be united to Him by a mutual indwelling ("you in me, and I in you," John 14:20).

Furthermore, this could be accomplished only if He left them, returned to the Father, and then sent the Spirit to indwell them too—His own Spirit who had been in His life from His mother Mary's womb until He rose again from the tomb and ascended to the Father.

To have the Holy Spirit indwelling us is the equivalent of having Jesus Himself indwelling us.

All this must have seemed strange indeed to the disciples. So now, as their Teacher, Jesus helps them understand both its meaning and its implications.

Who Am I?

How do you think about yourself? Or, to use the modern expression, what is your self-image? Do you think of yourself as somebody who is "in Christ," united to Him—someone in whom the Lord of glory dwells by His Holy Spirit?

When we first become Christians, it is usually because we see our need for forgiveness and new life. We realize that Christ is God's answer to that need. But it would be a mistake to think that the moment we come to faith we know everything there is to learn about being a Christian! It involves not only pardon and renewal but a new identity—it transforms who we are and how we think about ourselves. We still need to discover that "if anyone is in Christ, he is a new creation. The old has passed away; behold, the new has come" (2 Cor. 5:17).

To help His disciples grasp this, Jesus employs a familiar sight—a vine whose branches bear rich clusters of grapes.

Vines had been a common sight to God's people since they had settled the land (Josh. 24:13). In fact, they themselves had been described as a vine:

> You brought a vine out of Egypt;
>> you drove out the nations and planted it.
> You cleared the ground for it;
>> it took deep root and filled the land.
> The mountains were covered with its shade,
>> the mighty cedars with its branches.
> It sent out its branches to the sea
>> and its shoots to the River. (Ps. 80:8–11)

Commentators who think that the words of John 14:31 ("Rise, let us go from here") signal that Jesus and the disciples left the upper room to make their way through Jerusalem have wondered if what prompted His words was the sight of the Temple Vine. According to the Jewish tractate *Middoth*: "A vine of gold was standing over the entrance to the Sanctuary, and was suspended to the top of beams. Every one who vowed a leaf, or a berry, or a bunch, brought it and hung it up there."[1]

But where the disciples were is incidental to the teaching here. The important thing is its meaning. Jesus is using the vine imagery to teach them about the new reality the Spirit creates:

"I am the vine; you are the branches. You are nourished by your Spirit-effected union with Me. I am in you, and I give you life. You are in Me, and you draw on My resources to bear fruit for My Father's glory. In this relationship, the heavenly Father is like a vinedresser who cares for the vine. So, see the events and circumstances of your life as all part of His viticulture—including His use of His pruning knife—for He wants to see you become more fruitful!"

Several important principles are embedded in this picture.

The Source of Fruitfulness

The first principle is that fruitfulness—growth in our Christian life—depends on our union with the Lord Jesus. The branches depend on the Vine to produce good grapes.

Paul discovered this. He writes, "I can do all things through him [*en tō*, in him] who strengthens me" (Phil. 4:13). He does not mean he can do anything he sets his mind to—but because his life is "hidden with Christ in God" (Col. 3:3), resources are available to cope with anything. He thus knows how to handle wealth or poverty and exaltation or humiliation because he is "in Christ." Consequently, his life makes an impact on others, "bears fruit" in its influence on them, and points them to the Lord.

But fruitfulness will not occur if there is disease in the branches. Only clean, healthy branches bear good fruit. So it will be with the disciples. They have already been made clean by Jesus' word, and they will be further cleansed by pruning. Unless they continue to draw on His resources, they can do no good: "Apart from me you can do nothing" (John 15:5). So, they must "abide" in Him.

But what does it mean to "abide in Christ"? It would take a book to explain fully. But in the context of John 15, it means to live with a sense that the Son of God loves us and gave Himself for us, that He dwells within us by His Holy Spirit, and that we know that our life is now His and no longer our own. We believed *into* Christ (Paul uses that preposition to describe the union). All the resources embodied in Him are ours now, and we must draw on them.

We need to remind ourselves frequently, therefore, that we have been given a new identity in Him. I am a person who is in Christ now, someone in whom the Lord of glory has come to dwell.

Appreciating this transforms the way we think about ourselves, but also the way we think about and treat each other in the church. If, when we saw each other, we thought, "She is someone whom the Lord of glory is not ashamed to indwell!" would the logic of this not transform the way we treat each other? "Since Christ has so honored him, with what honor I should treat him too!" Then the fruitfulness of the early church would be repeated in our church family and people would be drawn to Christ by the very atmosphere of our fellowship.

The Pruning of the Father

Vinedressers prune their vines. Part of the genius of our Lord's illustration is its multifaceted nature. Vines grow through the influence of the soil, the sun, and the rain. But they also grow through the use of a pruning knife: "Every branch that does bear fruit he prunes, that it may bear more fruit" (John 15:2).

A friend in California once took me through his vineyards. The ground was strewn with a carpet of small twigs, the effects of his workers' knives—a myriad of evidences that it had been pruning season. But the knives had been used not to destroy but to fructify.

If we knew nothing about horticulture or gardening, the sight of someone cutting pieces off vines or bushes would seem like mindless destruction. But it is necessary for healthy growth—to produce a stronger plant and better fruit.

The branches of a vine cannot feel pain. Unlike them, we can. But like them, we do not understand all the Vinedresser is doing. So, when we are pruned, we ask questions: "Why is God doing this? Does He not care about me?" Our natural response to pruning is to say: "Please stop! Don't You see this is hurting me?"

But here Jesus helps us. True, understanding that the Father is a pruning-knife-using Vinedresser does not relieve the pain and solve every detail of life's mysteries. Our minds are far too finite to understand fully what the infinite Lord of all is doing. But if we grasp Jesus' teaching about our union with Him, we will realize that what to our eyes seems hurtful and even wasteful is essential for our spiritual development and usefulness. This is how God nurtures in us the fruit of the Spirit (Gal. 5:22–23).

Bishop Westcott expressed it well: "Everything is removed from the branch which tends to divert the vital power from production of fruit."[2] By cutting away what hinders our growth, He makes us more like Christ and more useful in His service.

This was a lesson Amy Carmichael (1867–1951) had to learn for herself and often taught others. A missionary in India for more than half a century, she saw and personally experienced much suffering. But reflecting on this passage, she wrote these wise words:

What prodigal waste it appears to be, to see scattered on the floor the bright green leaves, and the bare stem bleeding in a hundred places from the sharp knife. But with a tried and trusted husbandman there is not a random stroke in it at all; nothing cut away which it would not have been a loss to keep, and gain to lose.[3]

And she prayed: "Rid me, good Lord, of every diverting thing."

When the Vinedresser uses His pruning knife, the effects can be sore, and His ultimate purposes hidden. But He never makes a mistake. Not a cut is ever wasted. Jesus could have repeated here His earlier words to Simon Peter: "What I am doing you do not understand now, but afterward you will understand" (John 13:7).

What was true of the washing of Peter's feet is true of every cut of the divine pruning knife.

The Nourishment of the Word

Jesus adds a third important principle: union with Christ is nourished by His Word. "Already you are clean because of the word that I have spoken to you" (John 15:3).

Jesus had already assured His disciples that they were "clean." But if the channels of their union with Christ are to remain clean, so that their prayer requests correspond with God's will, the disciples must continue to make room for the word of Christ to work in them: "If you abide in me, and my words abide in you, ask whatever you wish, and it will be done for you" (v. 7).

These are significant words because they indicate what is involved in abiding in Christ.

Just at this point, however, interpretations of Jesus' words can go adrift. We must resist the temptation to see the word "abide" and then take our eye off the page. You may have attended a group Bible study in which the whole discussion wandered off track because someone said, "The way I like to think about 'abiding in Christ' is . . ." But how we "like to think" is not the relevant factor! Instead, we need to ask the text itself, "What do you think?" Usually, when we keep our focus on the passage, its details will become clear. That is true here. For Jesus Himself tells us how to "abide": the way to abide in Him is by letting His Word abide in us.

There is a pattern here that we find elsewhere in the New Testament. Paul writes about union with Christ in these terms: "As you received Christ Jesus the Lord, so walk in him . . ." (Col. 2:6). But how do we do this? His answer occurs a chapter later on: "Let the word of Christ dwell in you richly . . ." (Col. 3:16).

So, if you want to dwell in Christ, let the Word of Christ dwell in you richly. Leave no room in your life locked, no cupboard door closed to it. Let it bring light into your mind; let it warm your affections for Christ; let it subdue your will to His. The Word of Christ is the instrument of Christ, used by the Spirit of Christ, to nurture union with Christ and to transform us into the image of Christ. It is in this way that "we all, with unveiled face, beholding the glory of the Lord, are being transformed into the same image from one degree of glory to another. For this comes from the Lord who is the Spirit" (2 Cor. 3:18).

Before we leave this principle, there is one further aspect of it we should notice.

Sometimes an invisible disease enters a Christian's bloodstream. He or she is encouraged to think this way: our Bible study (whether in preaching or in small groups or individually) teaches us what we are to do. We then go and do it.

Of course, there are commands in Scripture. We have already heard Jesus Himself say, "If you know these things, blessed are you if you do them" (John 13:17). Obedience is essential.

But we must never lose sight of the fact that the Word itself does its own work in us. Thus Jesus had said: "You are clean because of the word that I have spoken to you" (15:3). Later on, His prayer takes up the same theme: "Sanctify them in the truth; your word is truth" (17:17).

The central lesson? Growth in holiness involves our doing what God's Word tells us. But more fundamental than our doing God's Word is what God's Word is doing to us! Yes, we are called to be "up and doing" for Him. But that is possible only when we have let the Word of God do its own work in us.

Paul expresses this same principle to the Thessalonians. He rejoiced that they had accepted the Word of God "not as the word of men but as what it really is, the word of God, which is at work in you believers" (1 Thess. 2:13).

This is why it is so important for us to sit under a steady ministry of the Word of God, to encourage those who preach to us to feed us well, and to pray for God's blessing on their expositions. Any preacher worth his salt will delight in having hearers whose disposition says: "Feed me more! I want the Word of Christ to dwell in me richly, in order that my fellowship and union with Christ may bear more fruit."

If this is lacking, we become anemic. But we may not notice our weakness for some time. We adjust to the spiritual diet we are being fed and become accustomed to it as though it is normal—and then we tend to assume we are living normal Christian lives. Only if we find ourselves in a situation where the Word of God is expounded well and fully does it dawn on us that we have been surviving on a starvation diet. Don't allow that to happen to you!

We have seen three important principles: the first, that our union with Christ is the source of our fruitfulness; the second, that this union will involve being pruned by the Father; the third, that it needs to be nourished by the Word. Now there is a final principle.

The Priority of Love

The basic fruit that grows in the soil of our union with the Lord Jesus is love.

You may be weary of hearing people say, "We must all love each other." It all sounds very vague. And sometimes it means little more than this: "If you loved me, you would let me be and do whatever I want to. And you certainly wouldn't tell me my behavior is wrong."

But listen to what Jesus says: "As the Father has loved me, so have I loved you. Abide in my love. If you keep my commandments, you will abide in my love, just as I have kept my Father's commandments and abide in his love" (John 15:9–10).

According to Jesus, true love for Him leads to keeping His commandments, just as His love for His heavenly Father led to His obedience to His commandments. Jesus Himself loved and obeyed the Ten Commandments!

Our Lord's encouragement to love does not reduce His demands on us. If anything, the reverse is the case, because the new measure of our love is this: "Love one another as I have loved you" (15:12). And how did He love them? "He loved them to the end" (13:1). He was going to "lay down his life for his friends" (15:13).

Yet notice that His commands are filled with grace. He gives them to His "friends." They were His disciples and servants. They had no right to know what the Master's intentions were. But now He is sharing His plans with them. Now they have become "friends." He had chosen them and called them—to be His friends. That is grace. That should spur us on to obedience.

In addition, He had introduced them to His own "best friend," the Holy Spirit. He was now going to send Him to them. It was within this fellowship that His Word would do its cleansing and sanctifying work in them.

"Yes," Jesus says, "I know that on your own you cannot produce this rich fruit of love; nor can you yield your lives to the heavenly Father so that your prayers correspond to His will. But united to Me, indwelt by the Spirit, no longer being orphans but now friends—all this will be possible. So, My friends, I am telling you to love one another" (see 15:17).

Jesus promised them that their "fruit should abide."

It has. For we are part of that fruit!

But long before that fruit, another fruit of the Spirit would be produced in the disciples. For being united to Him by grace, abiding in Him by faith, and letting His Word indwell them in obedience leads to joy: "These things I have spoken to you, that my joy may be in you, and that your joy may be full" (15:11).

Did Jesus mean He had said these things so that His disciples might be the source of His joy? Or did He mean that He would be the source of their joy? Almost certainly the latter. But in fact, both are true. Either way, their joy will be full.

8
—

Hated but Helped

John 15:18–27

"If the world hates you, know that it has hated me before it hated you. If you were of the world, the world would love you as its own; but because you are not of the world, but I chose you out of the world, therefore the world hates you. Remember the word that I said to you: 'A servant is not greater than his master.' If they persecuted me, they will also persecute you. If they kept my word, they will also keep yours. But all these things they will do to you on account of my name, because they do not know him who sent me. If I had not come and spoken to them, they would not have been guilty of sin, but now they have no excuse for their sin. Whoever hates me hates my Father also. If I had not done among them the works that no one else did, they would not be guilty of sin, but now they have seen and hated both me and my Father. But the word that is written in their Law must be fulfilled: 'They hated me without a cause.'

"But when the Helper comes, whom I will send to
you from the Father, the Spirit of truth, who proceeds
from the Father, he will bear witness about me. And
you also will bear witness, because you have been with
me from the beginning."

In his Gifford Lectures in Scotland in 1927–28, the
mathematician-philosopher Alfred North Whitehead stated
his view that "the safest general characterization of the European
philosophical tradition is that it consists of a series of footnotes to
Plato."[1] He meant that the central themes in Plato's writings had
set the course of discussion for centuries to come.

We might make a parallel statement and say that "the safest
general characterization of the narrative of the Bible is that it is a
series of footnotes to Genesis 3:15." There God says to the serpent
who has led Adam and Eve into sin, "I will put enmity between
you and the woman, and between your offspring and her offspring; he shall bruise your head, and you shall bruise his heel."

This conflict between the two offspring or seeds forms the
backbone of the Old Testament. Its story is one of many and varied conflicts: Cain seeks to destroy Abel; Potiphar's wife seeks to
destroy Joseph; Pharaoh seeks to destroy Moses; Goliath seeks to
destroy David; Babylon seeks to destroy Jerusalem.

The New Testament opens with the continuation of this conflict: Herod seeks to destroy Christ. It climaxes with the dramatic
conquest of "the dragon, that ancient serpent, who is the devil
and Satan" (Rev. 20:2). These are not isolated incidents but serial

episodes in the dramatic unfolding of the basic conflict between the Seed of the woman and the seed of the serpent.

The conclusion of this drama awaits the return of Christ. But it is already coming to its denouement in the upper room. Jesus knew the Father had given everything into His hands and that victory over the powers of darkness was secure. But He also knew that at this juncture of the battle, one of His own disciple band would betray Him. As He handed a morsel of bread to Judas, did He feel the serpent's eyes staring back at Him? For "Satan entered into him" (John 13:27).

Jesus had long known that these events would take place. During His earlier ministry, He had said "my time" or "the hour" had "not yet come" (2:4; 7:6, 8). But when, almost at the end of the Book of Signs, some Greeks asked "to see Jesus" it signaled to Him that the long-promised time when the gospel would break out into the gentile world had arrived. He responded: "Now is the judgment of this world; now will the ruler of this world be cast out. And I, when I am lifted up from the earth, will draw all people to myself." John adds, "He said this to show by what kind of death he was going to die" (12:30–33). The darkness was coming.

This makes all the more suggestive the possibility that the words in John 14:31, "Rise, let us go from here," have a military connotation: "Let us go forward to meet the enemy!"

The disciples were inevitably going to be caught up in the wake of this conflict. They were united to Him. It may well be that some of them sensed this already. But now Jesus was spelling it out clearly. Any subterranean vibrations they had previously felt were now being brought to the surface: they were going to be caught up in the conflict that had its epicenter in Him. Because they are Christ's, they will be hated. But because they are His, they will also be helped.

This is the simple theme of this section. Since the disciples are united to Christ like branches in a vine, in some measure they will share in His experience. But just as the Father cares for Him as the Vine, so He will care for them. Just as their Lord experienced the presence of the Holy Spirit as His Helper, so will they. But in addition, just as He experienced opposition, so will they.

Here, then, is a fundamental principle of discipleship. The Christian who does not anticipate opposition does not yet understand the nature of the Christian life.

We should be honest enough to admit that sometimes we experience opposition and criticism not because we are like Christ but because we are not. We Christians can be pigheaded, angular, and, sadly, sometimes too like the world that opposes the gospel. In that case, criticism and opposition may arise because we have behaved foolishly, inconsistently, and in an un-Christlike way.

But here Jesus is focusing attention on the opposition the disciples should expect because they belong to Him and are becoming like Him.

"If the world hates you . . ." is what grammarians call a "first class conditional" clause. The "if" does not mean "Maybe you will, maybe you won't be hated" but "Since you will be hated." It is inevitable that the bitter hatred of the serpent for the Seed will spill over onto His disciples.

John saw a dramatic representation of this in his vision on the island of Patmos. In it the serpent of Genesis 3 has grown into a great red dragon:

And a great sign appeared in heaven: a woman clothed with the sun, with the moon under her feet, and on her head a crown of twelve stars. She was pregnant and was crying out in birth pains and the agony of giving birth. And another sign appeared in heaven: behold, a great red dragon, with seven heads and ten horns, and on his heads seven diadems. His tail swept down a third of the stars of heaven and cast them to the earth. And the dragon stood before the woman who was about to give birth, so that when she bore her child he might devour it. She gave birth to a male child, one who is to rule all the nations with a rod of iron, but her child was caught up to God and to his throne, and the woman fled into the wilderness, where she has a place prepared by God, in which she is to be nourished for 1,260 days.

Now war arose in heaven, Michael and his angels fighting against the dragon. And the dragon and his angels fought back, but he was defeated, and there was no longer any place for them in heaven. And the great dragon was thrown down, that ancient serpent, who is called the devil and Satan, the deceiver of the whole world—he was thrown down to the earth, and his angels were thrown down with him. And I heard a loud voice in heaven, saying, "Now the salvation and the power and the kingdom of our God and the authority of his Christ have come, for the accuser of our brothers has been thrown down, who accuses them day and night before our God. And they have conquered him by the blood of the Lamb and by the word of their testimony, for they loved not their lives even unto death. Therefore, rejoice, O heavens and you who dwell in them! But woe to you, O earth and sea, for the devil has come down to you in great wrath, because he knows that his time is short!"

And when the dragon saw that he had been thrown down to the earth, he pursued the woman who had given birth to the male child. But the woman was given the two wings of the great eagle so that she might fly from the serpent into the wilderness, to the place where she is to be nourished for a time, and times, and half a time. The serpent poured water like a river out of his mouth after the woman, to sweep her away with a flood. But the earth came to the help of the woman, and the earth opened its mouth and swallowed the river that the dragon had poured from his mouth. Then the dragon became furious with the woman and went off to make war on the rest of her offspring, on those who keep the commandments of God and hold to the testimony of Jesus. And he stood on the sand of the sea. (Rev. 12:1–17)

In biblical times, people did not think of dragons as fire-breathing monsters of the kind slain by England's patron saint, George. They envisaged them as giant snakes—rather like the deadly Komodo dragons of Indonesia.

John describes how, when the dragon ("that ancient serpent, who is called the devil and Satan," 12:9) failed to destroy the Seed of the woman, he "became furious with the woman and went off to make war on the rest of her offspring, on those who keep the commandments of God and hold to the testimony of Jesus" (v. 17).

John was watching here what we might call the "movie version" of Jesus' words in the upper room. Christ has overcome the devil, but defeated foe though he is, he continues to fight, and will do so until he is thrown into the "lake of fire and sulfur" (20:10) and Eden is both restored and glorified (chs. 21–22). For now, although the serpent is powerless to destroy Christ, he will seek to destroy His friends, His church.

Sometimes we seem to have a very inadequate grasp of this. We are surprised by opposition. When there are internal struggles and strife in the church, we say, "Things like that don't happen in [evangelical!] churches like ours!" Our analysis of the situation is entirely horizontal, and individuals are blamed. Of course, we ourselves may be largely to blame. Yet we must also realize that union with Christ and faithfulness to Him will draw enemy fire. And, since our enemy has long experience of being "more crafty than any other beast of the field" (Gen. 3:1), he may use "friendly fire" too.

Alas for us, Satan constantly uses deception and lies. In keeping with his name *diabolos* (one who throws things, the accuser), he often lies hidden from us so that we fail to detect his hand in situations. We tend to analyze conflicts, difficulties, opposition in exclusively horizontal terms. We then begin to "fight and quarrel" (James 4:2)—in a mirror image of the world—and engage in a blame game instead of discerning the hand of the enemy seeking to destroy our church family.

This subtlety is illustrated in the following comments on a website listing the significance of baby names. Under the name Diabolos, which is still occasionally if rarely used for both boys and girls, it notes its meaning accurately but then makes light of it in its further comments:

The Given Name Diabolos

Diabolos is a form of Devil. See Devil for further details.

Embraced by many parents, the name Diabolos is one of warmth and cheerfulness.

Sweet yet mesmerizing, the name is a great blend of character and flair.

Although unique, your little chic Diabolos, is sure to make it a memorable one.[2]

"Warmth and cheerfulness. Sweet yet mesmerizing . . . chic Diabolos." Truly, the devil often appears as an angel of light (2 Cor. 11:14)!

So, we need to be awake, watchful, discerning.

Jesus now explains why.

Explanation

It was important that the disciples' hearts were not "troubled." But at the same time, they needed to take in, and to take seriously, the logic of Jesus' words: "If the world hates you, know that it has hated me before it hated you. If you were of the world, the world would love you as its own; but because you are not of the world, but I chose you out of the world, therefore the world hates you" (John 15:18–19).

These men experienced this from the very first days of the new covenant community. True, the promise of Jesus to send the Spirit (John 14:16) was fulfilled (Acts 2:33). Three thousand people were converted (Acts 2:41). The church became a vibrant new community, experiencing an outpouring of mutual love, and growing daily (Acts 2:42–47). But these words spoken in the upper room were also fulfilled. The pattern of the early church's life was one of blessings and beatings. When the gospel bears fruit, there will always be opposition to its fruitfulness.

The first days of the church in Jerusalem illustrate three fundamental tactics the devil seems to use repeatedly.

First there is intimidation, in the form of persecution (Acts 3–4).

When the church courageously stands firm, a second tactic is used: the ambitious seeking of reputation—as Ananias and Sapphira try to deceive their way into favor (Acts 5:1–11).

Then, when this fails because of the church's commitment to integrity, the serpent seeks to inject division into the practical outworking of the church's mercy ministry (Acts 6:1–7)—to which the church responds with practical wisdom. Failing in all three attacks, the devil simply goes back to the first one and tries again—only to discover that his "destruction" of Stephen actually leads to the conversion of Saul of Tarsus (Acts 7–9).

We must not allow ourselves to be outwitted by Satan. The principle here is "forewarned is forearmed." If we have read these chapters in Acts, we will not be "outwitted by Satan; for we are not ignorant of his designs" (2 Cor. 2:11). We will not expect our individual Christian lives or the community life of our church to be immune from opposition and antagonism so long as we are in this world.

Why not?

Because "you are not of the world" (John 15:19).

Is that hyper-pious? No, these are Jesus' words. We belong not to this world but to the new creation in Christ, a different order of reality (2 Cor. 5:17). Jesus is calling us simply to recognize who we are, to understand our new identity.

The more like the world we are, or our church is, the more we will be loved by the world—or at least tolerated as relatively harmless. But we will have lost our true identity and will make little impact on the world.

Jesus is telling His disciples that they—and we—should not expect to be loved by the world. Christians were persecuted in antiquity as belonging to a "new" or "third race"[3]—made welcome by neither gentile nor Jew. Those who are different from the world will be condemned by the world, but through them the world will be turned "upside down" (Acts 17:6)—or, more accurately, the right way up.

Do you ever think that perhaps the most difficult element in the gospel to take in is that we follow a crucified Savior? He meant it when He said that unless we take up the cross and follow Him, we cannot be His disciples. Here Jesus is underlining the reason: they crucified Him. They did so partly because they felt condemned by His life and speech. Their hostility was fueled by their guilt. It often is, as Jesus hints: "If I had not come and spoken to them, they would not have been guilty of sin, but now they have no excuse for their sin" (John 15:22). They felt condemned by His presence.

Yet, it was through their persecution of Him that the Seed bore fruit (12:24). If this was the pattern in the Master, it will be repeated in the servants (15:20).

Think about some parts of the world where becoming a Christian means being immediately recognizable as not belonging to "this world" and as a result suffering persecution (despite characteristically being among the best citizens). Yet it is often there that the gospel has borne rich fruit. Why? In large measure because there is evidence that Christ's disciples have become like their Master.

So it was in the early church when cross-bearing disciples rejoiced that they were counted "worthy" to suffer for the name of Jesus (Acts 5:41). The men who had been in the upper room must have looked back with gratitude that they had heard Jesus' warning: "Remember the word that I said to you: 'A servant is not greater than his master'" (John 15:20).

So, we need to reflect deeply on Jesus' syllogism:

Since	A servant is not greater than his master
and	I am your Master
and	They persecute Me
Therefore	They will persecute you also

This, then, is the reason disciples experience opposition. If so, how are they to be helped?

Unmasked

Jesus now makes an important move. He unmasks the opposition.

Opposition to our faith often seems so big, so strong, so determined, so insuperable. And the intended effect is that we will feel small, weak, and intimidated. Intimidation is a key weapon Satan uses to shut down Christian witness. Most of us shrink inwardly.

But Jesus is saying: "I want you to see this is not the reality of the situation. You need new lenses crafted for your spectacles so that you can see how great the kingdom of God is, and that it will triumph."

Remember how Elisha prayed? His servant went out one morning and discovered that Dothan, where they were, was surrounded by the Syrian army:

> And the servant said, "Alas, my master! What shall we do?" He said, "Do not be afraid, for those who are with us are more than those who are with them." Then Elisha prayed and said, "O LORD, please open his eyes that he may see." So the LORD opened the eyes of the young man, and he saw, and behold, the mountain was full of horses and chariots of fire all around. (2 Kings 6:15–17)

Jesus opens the disciples' eyes. He helps them see more clearly. In effect, He says: "Look at these people! Just look at them. You need to think clearly about who they are. You need to see them against the background of the greatness of God, the power of My resurrection, the sure advance of the kingdom, and the fact that what they do to harm and destroy I will use to build My church. If you see that, they will begin to shrink before your very eyes!"

First Principles

We need to learn to think about our lives in terms of first principles. Jesus draws the disciples' attention to three of them here:

First Principle 1: The Fatherhood of God

First, Jesus tells His disciples that those who persecute them do not know the Father, but they do: "All these things they will do to you on account of my name, because they do not know him who sent me" (John 15:21). How does this make a difference?

Opposition and intimidation make me feel small, marginalized, lonely. But I have a great privilege: I am a child of the heavenly Father. Sparrows sell for next to nothing, but not one of them is forgotten by God. I am much more valuable to Him than many sparrows (Luke 12:6–7)! I need not fear. He has a tender care for me and watches over me.

As the Heidelberg Catechism affirms, this is my "comfort in life and death":

I am not my own, but belong—
Body and soul, in life and in death—
to my faithful Savior, Jesus Christ.
He has fully paid for all my sins with his precious blood,
and has delivered me from the tyranny of the devil.
He also watches over me
in such a way that not a hair can fall from my head
without the will of my Father in heaven;
in fact, all things must work together for my salvation.
Because I belong to him, Christ, by his Holy Spirit,
also assures me of eternal life
and makes me wholeheartedly willing and ready from
now on
to live for him. (Q&A 1)

I could not be more secure!

Now I see those who are antagonistic to my faith no longer as giants but as people to be pitied, who know nothing of the grace of God in the gospel. By comparison with my heavenly Father, they are small and insignificant. They are powerless to do anything to me that He is not able to use for my ultimate good.

A memory from childhood comes back to me in this context. As young boys, we used to play football (soccer!) in our street. The father of one of my friends had played for a Scottish professional soccer team. Sometimes he came home early from work while we were still playing—and joined the losing team! If he joined your side, you knew—no matter how many goals behind you might be—that you would win the game! No team could hold out against my friend's father!

So it is with the friends of Jesus Christ the Son of the "Father of infinite majesty."[4] He is our Father and we are now His children—we have not been left orphans! This gives peace and poise. Those who seek to destroy the faith and fruit of His children do not realize that everything they do to harm them will be transformed by the heavenly Father into an instrument to do good:

> No weapon that is fashioned against you shall succeed,
>   And you shall refute every tongue that rises against
>   you in judgment.
> This is the heritage of the servants of the LORD
>   and their vindication from me, declares the LORD.
>   (Isa. 54:17)

First Principle 2: The Judgment of God.

Jesus adds: "If I had not come and spoken to them [His opponents], they would not have been guilty of sin, but now they have no excuse for their sin. Whoever hates me hates my Father also. If I had not done among them the works that no one else did, they would not be guilty of sin, but now they have seen and hated both me and my Father"(John 15:22–24).

All intimidating "giants" will face the righteous judgment of the God of heaven. Evidence against them will be brought into court. It will include the way they responded to the words and works of the Lord Jesus and to His disciples.

What did Jesus mean by saying that if He had not spoken or acted these people "would not have been guilty of sin" (vv. 22, 24)? He is speaking law court language here. In their case, His self-revelation—and their rejection of it—secures a "guilty" verdict. The manifestation of grace in Christ has exposed their crime.

The shining of the sun can cause flowers to open and give off the sweetest aromas. But it can also dry up polluted water so that it gives off a noxious stench. The shining of Christ the Sun of Righteousness has the same effect spiritually: disciples bear the good fruit of the Spirit; but the hearts of others are hardened and their hostility to God becomes evident.

Paul echoes this when he speaks about opposition to the gospel as "evidence of the righteous judgment of God" (2 Thess. 1:5) and of the Christian's poise in response to persecutors as "a clear sign to them of their destruction" (Phil. 1:28).

"We must all appear before the judgment seat of Christ" (2 Cor. 5:10). Disciples must learn to view their present experience in the light of the future. Doing so has the effect of shrinking things that seem big and puncturing the pride of man. It puts suffering persecution in a different light: "So we do not lose heart. . . . For this light momentary affliction is preparing for us an eternal weight of glory beyond all comparison, as we look not to the things that are seen but to the things that are unseen. For the things that are seen are transient, but the things that are unseen are eternal" (4:16–18).

Such a vision brought stability to the martyr Stephen, in the face of the overwhelming opposition that had been mounted against his witness: "Behold, I see the heavens opened, and the Son of Man standing at the right hand of God" (Acts 7:56).

So, we must learn—whenever an intimidating "giant" threatens us—to look beyond him (or her) and see that behind the giant is the shadow of the judgment seat of Christ. In its light the giant will become a dwarf. The road on which the giant now travels leads only to a lost eternity.

This brings us to a third "first principle" that secures us in the face of opposition.

First Principle 3: Unsurprised

If first principle number one is that we know the Father, while those who persecute the church do not, and principle number two is that the enemies of Christ will face judgment, the third is that when disciples encounter opposition they are able to say, "I am not surprised; I have been expecting you."

Never be surprised that there is opposition. Yes, it may come from unexpected and surprising sources. But no matter its human origin, we should not be surprised by the fact itself. Why not? Jesus explains: if He was opposed, then opposition to those who trust and follow Him is inevitable.

In learning this principle lies great strength. It makes all the difference when we face temptation from Satan, or experience opposition from non-Christians, or encounter self-seeking individuals in the church whose behavior threatens the fellowship.

We are able to say: "I did not know from what corner opposition would come. I could not predict with any certainty what specific form it would take. But I knew it would come. I was expecting it. I have not been taken by surprise, and I am ready."

When this is true, opposition does not send us into panic. It does not make us wring our hands and say, "What is going wrong? Surely things like this shouldn't be happening to me, and to our church!" We are not so naive as to think: "Why is it that they're opposing somebody like me? I'm just trying to live a normal Christian life. I have never done them any harm!" No. We expect it. We are not surprised. We are not sent into a panic, because we know that the Lord Jesus is not in a panic about this opposition to Him and therefore to us as well. So long as we remember that the opposition is not, ultimately, about us, but about Christ, all will be well. We will be able to say: "Lord, this is about You. And I know You can deal with it."

When this is true of us, it is Christ's opponents who will be taken by surprise! They naturally assume (since they are so often intimidators) that we will be overcome and easily broken down. They believe themselves to be smarter, more powerful in debate, more "modern" and "civilized" than Christians. Of course, they are often skilled in making us look and feel small. But since they do not believe in Christ, they do not reckon with the power of the gospel, or with the presence of the Helper. They do not know what "makes Christians tick"; and they know nothing about the principle articulated by John Bunyan (who knew all about demeaning opposition):

He that is down needs fear no fall,
He that is low no pride;

135

He that is humble ever shall
Have God to be his guide.[5]

We are children of the heavenly Father. We have a great God
who protects us. We have been taught by the Lord Jesus to anticipate opposition. We know that it is ultimately directed against
Him, not us. And so, like Stephen, when opposed, we are suffi-
ciently set free from intimidation that we are able to pray, "Lord,
do not hold this sin against them" (Acts 7:60).
One final emphasis in this section should be noted.

Witness

The closing words of John 15 may, at first sight, seem almost out
of place, for Jesus now speaks again about the Holy Spirit (who
has not been mentioned in it thus far). Earlier Jesus had spoken
about Him as the disciples' *paraklētos* or "Helper" (14:16, 26).
Now He returns to the same theme, and develops it further: "But
when the Helper comes, whom I will send to you from the Father,
the Spirit of truth, who proceeds from the Father, he will bear witness about me. And you also will bear witness, because you have
been with me from the beginning" (John 15:26–27).
What does He mean? The main points are clear enough:
The Helper will come, and He will bear witness about Christ.
The disciples will also bear witness about Christ.
These words, like Jesus' earlier teaching on the Spirit, are both
a promise and a prophecy. They had their first fulfillment on the
day of Pentecost. The Apostles bore witness to Christ (Acts 2:4).
Peter in particular did this at length (vv. 14–36).
But what made their witness so effective (three thousand

professed faith that day)? Not Peter's biblical theology (although he had certainly learned a great deal in Jesus' "postresurrection seminars," Acts 1:3). Nor was it his eloquence—although, even if he was an "uneducated, common" person (4:13), there was real gospel eloquence in his preaching. It was the coming of the Holy Spirit. He bore His witness to Jesus through their witness to Him.

Notice the way in which Jesus embeds a parallelism into His words:

The disciples bear witness.

What gives their witness authority?

They have been with Him "from the beginning."

In fact, they are Jesus' closest "friends" (John 15:15).

Therefore, each of them is qualified to be Jesus' *paraklētos*!

But they are not alone in having been with Jesus from the beginning.

The Holy Spirit "will bear witness about me" (15:26).

What gives His witness authority?

He also has been with Jesus "from the beginning."

In fact, He is Jesus' closest "friend."

Therefore, He is qualified to be Jesus' *paraklētos*.

In fact, the Spirit has been with the Lord Jesus longer than the disciples have been. In His case, "from the beginning" is long before the "beginning" of their knowledge of Him. He has been with Him since He was in His mother's womb. But there is a "beginning" that goes further back than even His conception in Mary's womb. For the Spirit whom Jesus will "send . . . from the Father" is the Witness who "proceeds from the Father" (15:26). And this procession is from eternity!

Notice the difference in the tense of the verbs "send" and "proceed."

The sending lies in the future (on the day of Pentecost).

The proceeding is in the present.

Throughout the ages, the best expositors of Scripture have taken this procession to refer not simply to the *economic* relation between the Spirit and the Father—His coming in history—but to the *ontological*, the eternal relationship between Them: the Spirit always, from all eternity, *proceeds* from the Father.

Jesus is pointing the disciples back to a "time when time was not." In this night of crisis, He is drawing back the curtain on the mystery of the Trinity. He is telling them that in Him they have been brought to know the Father with whom the Son ever lives face-to-face, and from whom the Spirit ever proceeds. Further-more, He is announcing that He Himself will send this same Spirit to them from the Father. He can only have authority to do that if He is God the Son. No mere man has authority to send God!

Are you still tracking with Jesus?

If any verses in the Bible are likely to convince us that the doctrine of the Trinity matters, it is surely these. It is often thought to be the most speculative and least practical of all Christian doctrines, but the truth must be the reverse. Otherwise, why would Jesus teach these things in a time of crisis? In fact—if we can only grasp its significance—the Trinity must be the most fundamental and the most practical of all biblical truths.

Here, in this dark hour, Jesus is casting an anchor for His disciples into the very heart of the being of God. It is as though He is saying: "My friends, I know the opposition may be fierce. But do not let your hearts be troubled. Trust in Me. And bear witness to Me, no matter what. Be on your guard and ready for persecution, even hatred. But do not think your adversaries' resources are greater than yours. Keep on being My witnesses. You are not alone. The Helper is with you. He will come to indwell you. And remember this: Like you, He was with Me from the beginning of My ministry. But (unlike you) He was with Me from an earlier beginning—when I, the Word, became flesh. Indeed, He was with Me from an even earlier beginning—from the beginning that had no beginning, 'in the beginning' when I was 'at the Father's side' (John 1:1, 18), when all that existed was 'in the beginning, God' (Gen. 1:1)."

To borrow an expression used by C.S. Lewis, we might say that the disciples are being given access to "deep magic from the dawn of time."[6] When the Helper comes to them, they will be resourced by heaven and anchored to God the Trinity. Before Him all human opposition shrinks.

And so, instead of being intimidated and crushed, these young men would be emboldened. They were sent to "all nations" as witnesses (Luke 24:47–48). The rest of the New Testament tells us they did in fact go, and the traditions of the church tell us they were willing to give their lives for the Savior.

Nor would it be long before they would see Jesus' promise fulfilled in someone who was not present with them in the upper room, when their colleague Stephen was martyred. This apparent defeat became the means by which another young man, at whose feet his murderers laid their garments, would become a witness of Christ to the nations.

Thus, in the conversion of Saul of Tarsus, a new stage of witness began—and it became clear that the promises Jesus gave in the upper room would continue to be fulfilled until the end of time. Before we move on, we should pause to reflect on, and give thanks for, a privilege we have not thus far noticed. In our reading of these chapters in John's gospel, we are experiencing the effect of Jesus' promise that "the Spirit of truth, who proceeds from the Father, he will bear witness about me. And you also will bear witness. . . ."

In addition to everything else, this was a promise to the Apostles that they would be enabled by the Spirit to provide for the church in every age their ultimate witness to Christ—the New Testament. Here, supremely, is the joint witness of the Apostles and the Holy Spirit. And since they were with Christ from the beginning—the beginning of His ministry in the case of the Apostles, the beginning of His life in the case of the Holy Spirit, we can rely on their words.

As we look back now on John 13–15, we are indeed grateful for the teaching Jesus has already given. And there is still more to come.

But why did Jesus give all this teaching to the Apostles only then, in the upper room? The next chapter opens with the answer to that question.

9

Why? Why? Why?

John 16:1–16

"I have said all these things to you to keep you from falling away. They will put you out of the synagogues. Indeed, the hour is coming when whoever kills you will think he is offering service to God. And they will do these things because they have not known the Father, nor me. But I have said these things to you, that when their hour comes you may remember that I told them to you.

"I did not say these things to you from the beginning, because I was with you. But now I am going to him who sent me, and none of you asks me, 'Where are you going?' But because I have said these things to you, sorrow has filled your heart. Nevertheless, I tell you the truth: it is to your advantage that I go away, for if I do not go away, the Helper will not come to you. But if I go, I will send him to you. And when he comes, he will convict the world concerning sin and righteousness and judgment: concerning sin, because they do not believe in me; concerning righteousness, because I go to the Father, and you will see me no longer; concerning judgment, because the ruler of this world is judged.

"I still have many things to say to you, but you cannot bear them now. When the Spirit of truth comes, he will guide you into all the truth, for he will not speak on his own authority, but whatever he hears he will speak, and he will declare to you the things that are to come. He will glorify me, for he will take what is mine and declare it to you. All that the Father has is mine; therefore I said that he will take what is mine and declare it to you.

"A little while, and you will see me no longer; and again a little while, and you will see me."

Perhaps time seemed to stand still in the upper room. Certainly, it must have gone into slow motion for the disciples as they watched Jesus wash their feet. Apart from Peter's opening outburst, the embarrassed silence in the room was probably deafening.

How many times did Jesus need to return to the containers to fill the basin with fresh water? Did He say anything apart from His words to Peter? Did Judas say anything at all? John leaves all these details to our imagination; however interesting they might be, they are not important for us to know. Only two things are important: what Jesus did—wash the disciples' feet and give a morsel of bread to Judas and dismiss him—and what Jesus said.

Like the foot washing, the Master's teaching was personal, intimate, and full of grace. The whole evening was one of cleansing. He cleansed His disciples' feet by pouring water over them; He cleansed their lives by pouring His word into them (John 15:3).

We have just been reflecting on a profound part of that cleansing word—amazing though it may seem, Jesus chose this moment to talk about the Trinity.

This in itself must have made what He goes on to say seem almost unbelievable to the disciples: "I still have many things to say to you, but you cannot bear them now"(16:12).

Really? He had just finished speaking to them about what theologians call the ontological and economic Trinity! What more could He say? You would have every sympathy for any disciple who interjected, "Lord, I can't take any more!"

Jesus has not finished teaching them. But He has taken them as far as they are able to go in their understanding—for the moment ("now"). Later, as the Spirit takes up His teaching role, there will be more to learn. "Afterward you will understand" (13:7).

Jesus was a wise and self-disciplined Teacher, and there is a great deal we can learn from Him here.

Some people love to teach. Some people love to study in order to be able to teach. But these two things do not in themselves qualify us to teach in the church. Something more is required: loving the people, and therefore wanting to serve them by using the gift of teaching. After all, Christ has given that gift not for our sake but for theirs.

Without this, our teaching can easily dissolve into a means of self-gratification disguised as ministry. It may perhaps inform and instruct—and even do it well—but something will be lacking: the spiritual nourishment that marked Jesus' teaching and that of the Apostles. That nourishment comes when the teacher is, as it were, on his knees, Jesus-like, and when the disposition he exhibits says, "The Lord loves you, and He has given me something to pass on to you because I love you too and want to serve you."

The Apostle Paul saw this, and he reflected on it in three telling comments: "What we proclaim is not ourselves, but Jesus Christ as Lord, with ourselves as your servants for Jesus' sake" (2 Cor. 4:5); "So, being affectionately desirous of you, we were ready to share with you not only the gospel of God but also our own selves, because you had become very dear to us" (1 Thess. 2:8); "The aim of our charge is love" (1 Tim. 1:5).

The original model of this spirit is seen in the mixture of love and patience expressed in Jesus' words: "I still have many things to say to you, but you cannot bear them now" (John 16:12).

It is against this background that Jesus now seems to be answering the disciples' unspoken questions as though He knew what they were thinking. He did because He had perfect discernment.

Discernment is an important element in giving spiritual counsel. It means not only understanding what people say and the questions they ask but understanding the people themselves and "the question behind the questions." Jesus answered not only the questions but the questioners. As John tells us, "he himself knew what was in man" (2:25).

The greater a person's understanding of Scripture, experience of the ways of God, and spiritual sensitivity, the more this will be true of the person. In Jesus' perfect humanity, we find such knowledge, understanding, and sensitivity in perfect balance. Here He patiently, carefully, and lovingly answers questions that perhaps the disciples were simply too embarrassed to ask. Perhaps they were scarcely able to articulate them even to themselves.

That would be understandable. Jesus was stretching them to the limit (after all, He has just stretched our understanding to the limit in what He says about the relationships within the Trinity). So, He answers three questions:

Why, Jesus, are You telling us this?

Why, Jesus, are You telling us now? and,

Why, Jesus, are You telling us that You are leaving us?

Why Tell Us This?

The first question is immediately answered: "I have said all these things to you to keep you from falling away" (John 16:1).

Our Lord had multiple goals for His teaching, and so His ministry of the Word of God functions at different levels and has a variety of effects.

Earlier, we learned one of these effects is joy: "These things I have spoken to you, that my joy may be in you, and that your joy may be full" (15:11). Now He is balancing that by emphasizing why His teaching on the coming suffering and the Spirit's help is particularly important. It will protect the disciples from "falling away" and from abandoning Him the way Judas had just done. It forewarns them of danger and equips them to face it—for they will soon enough find themselves confronted by hostility in the synagogues; people will feel justified in persecuting and even killing them and will perversely believe they are serving God by doing so (16:1–2).

Notice what He says: Jesus provides an explanation. The disciples need to grow in discernment. What they will see and feel is one thing. But they need to be able to penetrate behind appearances: "They will do these things because they have not known the Father, nor me" (16:3).

This is an important lesson to learn. Jesus is saying: "Persecution will be directed against you, but it is not ultimately about you!"

When we understand that, even though the pain of persecution remains, the poison is drawn out of its sting. We are able to say: "Lord, this is really about You, not about me. And so, I commit this burden to You. You are able to carry it—and me!" This is what produces a measure of poise.

Jesus also provides an advance warning: "I have said these things to you, that when their hour comes [i.e., the hour of the kingdom of darkness] you may remember that I told them to you" (16:4).

We have heard this lesson before: forewarned is forearmed. Opposition arises, but we are not overwhelmed by it because it does not take us by surprise. We can say, "I knew you were coming even if I didn't know from what quarter you would come." We are not dislodged. We are guarded by Jesus' warning words and thus prevented from falling away.

But what were "these things" that Jesus had said to reassure them?

First of all: "Let not your hearts be troubled" (14:1, 27). You have good reason not to be. "Believe in God [trust Him]; believe also in me [trust Me too]" (v. 1).

Second: "I will ask the Father, and he will give you another Helper, to be with you forever" (v. 16). He will be your Counselor, giving you wisdom. And He will be with you so that you will never be silenced: "He will bear witness about me. And you also will bear witness" (15:26–27).

We should pause to underline again the principle illustrated here. Jesus' word will effect in His disciples the very transformation to which it points them. Here again we see the word of Christ at work. It accomplishes what it commands. Our task is to make room for it. For if it dwells in us, we have resources to sustain us; a bulwark is created within us that can withstand opposition. We grow in the discernment that enables us to see what lies behind it, and we will receive the wisdom we need to deal with it.

This is why Jesus is pouring His word into His disciples' minds and hearts. He is giving them the resources that will prevent them from falling away.

But why is Jesus saying these things now?

Why Tell Us This *Now*?

You can imagine the disciples thinking: "Why did You not tell us this before now, Jesus?"

Jesus responds: "I have said these things to you, that when their hour comes you may remember that I told them to you. I did not say these things to you from the beginning, because I was with you" (John 16:4–5).

Perhaps you have had the experience of giving bad news to someone you love. Your heart breaks for them. You want to safeguard them. You feel the weight of the sadness. If you could, you would carry the burden yourself. But you know that you must share the news.

Jesus had carried His heavy burden for years, but the cross was now an imminent reality. Several times, He had told the disciples what awaited Him—and them—but in large measure He had protected them. He knew better than they did just how fragile they were. They would not have been able to take the strain.

This, then, was why He had delayed fuller disclosure until now—not for His sake but for theirs. He wanted to protect them. He could do that because He was with them Himself (16:4b). But now He was leaving them, and they needed to be told more.

It would have been self-deception for the disciples to think that if they had known the future, they would have lived differently. They had known enough—and they knew more now—but it made relatively little impact. They probably did not realize the extent to which Jesus had protected them—or even that they had needed His protection (at times Peter seemed to think he could protect Jesus!).

It surely fills us with admiration when we see the way Jesus bore on His own all the strain of what awaited Him at the end of His ministry, and He also protected His disciples from a burden they would not have been able to bear. As Isaiah says, "He will tend his flock like a shepherd; he will gather the lambs in his arms; he will carry them in his bosom" (Isa. 40:11).

When our children are young, we carry them. But the time comes when they need to learn to walk. Some will fret and still want to be carried. But they must learn. So here. The disciples need to learn to walk on a dangerous path without Jesus' physical presence to guide and guard them. He will be with them in the person of His Spirit. But they will need to trust Him. There will be sufficient grace for them in their time of need. But tomorrow's grace does not arrive today.

This is the answer to the question, "Why did You not tell us all this before now?" Sufficient to each day is its own evil—and sufficient for the day is the grace provided on that day. This is the life of faith.

Why Leave Now?

A third question arises: "If this is what is going to befall us, Jesus, why are You leaving us now?"

Now He tells them more bluntly what He had already taught them, but they had not really understood: "I tell you the truth: it is to your advantage that I go away, for if I do not go away, the Helper will not come to you. But if I go, I will send him to you" (John 16:7).

How counterintuitive these words must have sounded! How could He be telling them that they were entering this period of crisis—but He was leaving them? How could this possibly be to their advantage?

The answer, as we have seen, is that only when He has finished His work and ascended to the throne of heaven will He send His Spirit to them. Perhaps we can think of it this way: only when He has become the "complete" Savior we need will He have provided for the Spirit the equipment He needs to transform His followers fully into His likeness.

But there is a more immediate sense in which the coming of the Spirit will be to the advantage of the disciples: "And when he comes, he will convict the world concerning sin and righteousness and judgment: concerning sin, because they do not believe in me; concerning righteousness, because I go to the Father, and you will see me no longer; concerning judgment, because the ruler of this world is judged" (16:8–11).

Spirit of Conviction

We usually think of these words as a general promise and apply them immediately to the present day. They certainly have a contemporary application. But once again, we need to curb the instinct to leap over twenty centuries to arrive at our own time. For, in the first instance, Jesus' words constitute a specific prophecy. Within a matter of weeks, the disciples would witness their fulfillment—on the day of Pentecost—as a result of Peter's sermon.

In fact, what happened on the day of Pentecost was virtually a phrase-by-phrase fulfillment of Jesus' prophecy:

1. On the day of Pentecost, the Spirit convicted "the world" (John 16:8). In John's vocabulary, "the world" has the nuance "not only Jews, but people from the gentile world"—like those who were gathered in Jerusalem: "Men from every nation under heaven" who would hear the gospel preached to them in the native languages of the "Parthians and Medes and Elamites and residents of Mesopotamia, Judea and Cappadocia, Pontus and Asia, Phrygia and Pamphylia, Egypt and the parts of Libya belonging to Cyrene, and visitors from Rome, . . . Cretans and Arabians" (Acts 2:5–11).

2. On the day of Pentecost, the Spirit convicted the world "concerning sin, because they do not believe in me" (John 16:9). Jesus is not saying that men become sinners only if they do not believe in Him. Rather, He means that on the day of Pentecost, their guilt for not believing on Him will be made abundantly clear. The Spirit will act as both the counsel for the defense of Jesus and the prosecuting counsel of sinners to show them this is the case.

Peter's preaching on the day of Pentecost had a courageous directness. He charged his hearers, "This Jesus . . . you crucified and killed . . ." (Acts 2:23). They had refused to believe in Him and had condemned Him and treated Him as a guilty criminal and crucified Him. But God had pronounced the final verdict on

Him, for He "raised him up, loosing the pangs of death" (v. 24). Now their sinfulness stood exposed. They were sinners; they had rejected God's Messiah. Convicted of their sin of unbelief, "they were cut to the heart, and said to Peter and the rest of the apostles, 'Brothers, what shall we do?' And Peter said to them, 'Repent . . .'" (vv. 37–38). No wonder.

3. On the day of Pentecost, the Spirit convicted "concerning righteousness, because I go to the Father, and you will see me no longer" (John 16:10). Why is the fact that Jesus went to the Father the reason the Spirit convicts concerning righteousness? Is this conviction of their lack of righteousness? Perhaps partly. But more is involved. The Spirit brings conviction because of something that is true of Jesus—His "going to the Father"—that is, His death, burial, resurrection, and ascension (see 14:12, 28; again in 16:28).

Throughout John's gospel, Jesus has been on trial before the watching world. John has brought forward various defense witnesses: the woman at the well (ch. 4); the paralyzed man at the pool of Bethesda (ch. 5); the man born blind (ch. 9); Lazarus (ch. 11), among others. In different ways, they all gave testimony to Jesus' true identity and His righteousness. In the face of this evidence, however, as His "trial" moves toward a verdict, the One delivered by Judas, Annas, Caiaphas, Herod, the Roman garrison, the mob, and Pontius Pilate will be pronounced "guilty."

But now the Spirit Himself is giving testimony. Jesus' resurrection and ascension constitute His vindication by the Spirit (as Paul notes in Rom. 1:4 and 1 Tim. 3:16). They demonstrate Christ's righteousness. God declared in His resurrection and now proclaims by the outpouring of the Spirit that Jesus is the

Righteous One! Those who crucified Him were wrong. And now, in this demonstration of Christ's righteousness, the Spirit convicts them of their unrighteousness.

4. On the day of Pentecost, the Spirit convicted "concerning judgment, because the ruler of this world is judged" (John 16:11). Many of those gathered in Jerusalem had despised Jesus' claim that God had placed all judgment into His hands (5:22). But at the cross, "the ruler of this world" had been judged, just as Jesus had promised: "Now is the judgment of this world; now will the ruler of this world be cast out" (12:31; see Col. 2:15–16). The one who engineered Christ's condemnation is now himself judged and condemned. The same fate must therefore await those who had sided with him against the Savior! Their situation was desperate!

Was there any hope for those who now stood convicted and condemned?

Yes, because the Spirit convicts in order to convert. If those who were convicted repented and believed in Christ, they could receive the sign of the washing away of their sins and of their reception into His family in baptism—forgiveness and new life could be theirs!

All this would indeed be to the "advantage" of the disciples on the day of Pentecost. Their number would multiply overnight from around 120 (Acts 1:15) to around 3,120 (2:41)! That was more or less exactly the "thirtyfold" increase Jesus had promised in the parable of the sower—the "sixtyfold" and the "hundredfold" were soon to follow (Matt. 13:8; see Acts 2:41, 47; 5:14; 6:1, 7).

But the coming of the Spirit would bring even greater advantages to the disciples.

Spirit of Illumination

Apostles though they were, these men still had much to learn; and Jesus still had much to teach them (John 16:12).

He may have been thinking of His postresurrection seminars during the forty days between Easter and Pentecost, when He taught them more "about the kingdom of God" (Acts 1:3). But apart from references to Jesus' appearance on Easter Sunday and His restoration of Peter (John 20–21), John's gospel makes no reference to these.

It seems likely, therefore, that Jesus has something else in mind, and He confirms this in the words that follow: "When the Spirit of truth comes, he will guide you into all the truth" (John 16:13).

Here, once again, we need to be careful not to leap out of the upper room directly into our own living rooms! Jesus was speaking not to us but to the Apostles. To understand these words, we must first ask, How was this promise fulfilled for them? Only then should we ask what the implications for us might be.

The Apostles who listened to Jesus that night were given a unique and unrepeatable role in the church.[1] There was no "succession plan" for them.

These considerations help us understand that what Jesus said to these men as Apostles carries implications for us, but His words were not spoken to us. Thus, when He says, "When the Spirit of truth comes, he will guide you into all the truth . . . ," we should not make the mistake of thinking that we are among the "you" He is directly addressing. We are not to expect direct revelation from the Holy Spirit. Instead, we should ask: "In what way did the Spirit keep this promise to the Apostles? And how, if at all, does this relate to the church today?"

Several clues point us to the answer. Jesus says that the Spirit will come to glorify Him (John 16:14). But how will He do this?

1. He will do this by taking what is Christ's and declaring it to the Apostles (16:14).

Can we still identify what the Spirit declared to them? Think back to the earlier scene in chapter 14. Remember how much Jesus emphasized the importance of His own words (14:10, 21, 23, 24, 25, 26). He also reassured the Apostles that the Spirit would teach them "all things" by reminding them of "all that I have said to you" (v. 26).

Is it becoming clearer where we might have access to this teaching? Yes, indeed! Jesus' words are virtually a prophecy of the way the Spirit would enable the Apostles to remember what He had said and preserve it in the four Gospels.

2. He will also do this by guiding them "into all the truth" (16:13).

Do we have access to this truth? Again, we do. But where? Reflect again on Jesus' words. They are virtually a prophecy of the events described in the Acts of the Apostles and the contents of the New Testament letters. In fact, Paul speaks about how the Ephesians had "learned Christ!—assuming that you have heard about him and were taught in him, as the truth is in Jesus . . ." (Eph. 4:20–21).

3. He will do this further by showing the Apostles "the things that are to come" (John 16:13). Do we have access to this too? Once again, yes! But where? In the prophecies recorded in various books of the New Testament and perhaps especially in the book of Revelation. Its first words are almost an echo of Jesus' words

in the upper room: "The revelation of Jesus Christ, which God gave him to show to his servants the things that must soon take place . . ." (Rev. 1:1).

Combine these clues, and what do we have? Gospels, Acts, Letters, and Revelation—the New Testament!

Included in the teaching Jesus is giving the disciples—and perhaps one of the things they would not be able to "bear" if He told them directly—is that a major part of their commission was, through the Spirit's ministry to and in them, to write the New Testament. They would bear witness to Him, and the Spirit would also bear witness—simultaneously. Through what the Spirit enabled them to write, He would continue to illumine darkened minds to recognize the face of Christ revealed in His written Word and enable deaf ears to hear His voice and come to trust in Him.

So, Jesus is speaking not to us but to the Apostles.

But although these words were not spoken to us, they have an application to us. For we too need to be led into the truth; we, too, need to know what our Savior said; we, too, need to know how to live in the light of what is still to come. And now that we have the New Testament, we can!

So, if we want to see the Christ who is glorified by the Spirit, what should we do? Just exactly what we are doing in reading John's gospel—meditating on the Scriptures and letting the Word of Christ dwell in us richly (Col. 3:16). In this way, the Spirit works inwardly in our minds today to illumine our understanding of who Jesus is and what He teaches us, and to learn how we in turn may honor and glorify Him!

To Your Advantage

Here, then, is another dimension of the "advantage" it is to the disciples that Jesus was leaving them and sending the Spirit in His place. In a sense, Jesus Himself had taught them "from the outside." They were "foolish . . . , and slow of heart to believe all that the prophets have spoken" (Luke 24:25). So are we. But the Lord has sent His Spirit to us. He not only revealed Christ in the pages of the written Word of God in the New Testament, but continues to indwell believers in order to illuminate their understanding "from the inside."

The disciples were filled with alarm. One of their fears was that if Jesus left them, they would feel far away from Him, their memories of Him would grow dim, and their knowledge of Him would diminish. But Jesus was promising that the reverse would be the case. He would be nearer to them than ever; His Spirit would refresh their memory of all He had taught them and would enable them to understand it; they would come to know Him even better. And because of this, one of them would be able to write to encourage all future disciples: "Though you have not seen him, you love him. Though you do not now see him, you believe in him and rejoice with joy that is inexpressible and filled with glory" (1 Peter 1:8).

It was, indeed, to their "advantage" that Jesus left them.

And—until we see Him face-to-face for the first time—it is to our advantage as well.

Christ still has many things to say to us too. But let us not be blind to how He will say them: let this Word of Christ, given to us in the pages of the New Testament, dwell in us richly!

Confusion before Clarity

John 16:17–33

So some of his disciples said to one another, "What is this that he says to us, 'A little while, and you will not see me, and again a little while, and you will see me'; and, 'because I am going to the Father'?" So they were saying, "What does he mean by 'a little while'? We do not know what he is talking about." Jesus knew that they wanted to ask him, so he said to them, "Is this what you are asking yourselves, what I meant by saying, 'A little while and you will not see me, and again a little while and you will see me'? Truly, truly, I say to you, you will weep and lament, but the world will rejoice. You will be sorrowful, but your sorrow will turn into joy. When a woman is giving birth, she has sorrow because her hour has come, but when she has delivered the baby, she no longer remembers the anguish, for joy that a human being has been born into the world. So

330, 000

also you have sorrow now, but I will see you again, and your hearts will rejoice, and no one will take your joy from you. In that day you will ask nothing of me. Truly, truly, I say to you, whatever you ask of the Father in my name, he will give it to you. Until now you have asked nothing in my name. Ask, and you will receive, that your joy may be full.

"I have said these things to you in figures of speech. The hour is coming when I will no longer speak to you in figures of speech but will tell you plainly about the Father. In that day you will ask in my name, and I do not say to you that I will ask the Father on your behalf; for the Father himself loves you, because you have loved me and have believed that I came from God. I came from the Father and have come into the world, and now I am leaving the world and going to the Father."

His disciples said, "Ah, now you are speaking plainly and not using figurative speech! Now we know that you know all things and do not need anyone to question you; this is why we believe that you came from God." Jesus answered them, "Do you now believe? Behold, the hour is coming, indeed it has come, when you will be scattered, each to his own home, and will leave me alone. Yet I am not alone, for the Father is with me. I have said these things to you, that in me you may have peace. In the world you will have tribulation. But take heart; I have overcome the world."

Professors who teach preaching and communication in seminaries emphasize how important it is to be understood.

Sometimes people say to preachers, "You need to preach much more simply so we can all understand—like Jesus preached!" But do you ever wonder how Jesus would have fared in a preaching class? His most faithful disciples had been listening to Him now for three years. He used no big words. But by no means was everything He said crystal clear to them. They were not lacking in intelligence. Yet even here, in the upper room, they had to ask Him what He meant—and they still found it puzzling. In addition, He said that there were things they needed to know that they were not yet able to bear (John 16:12).

Was Jesus a poor communicator? Far from it. We are told that "the great throng heard him gladly" (Mark 12:37). But that does not mean they understood Him. The two things are not the same.

The problem was not intellectual ability. Nor was it abstruse vocabulary or a lack of clarity. It was spiritual. The disciples did not have the insight, the spiritual understanding, or the discernment to grasp what Jesus was saying about the kingdom of God. They needed illumination. Only then would the truth dawn. Only then would they be able to say, "Now I see!"

The disciples were not yet at that point. They were still confused. What did Jesus mean by saying He was leaving them to go to the Father, but He was going to come back to them? What was all this talk about "a little while"? None of it seemed to make any sense; Jesus was speaking in riddles!

But something encouraging was beginning to happen. In their perplexity, they had begun to talk among themselves: "What does He mean? I don't understand Him; do you?" "No, I don't either. I am confused."

Perhaps you have had the experience of tidying a room, but in the process you realize you created more mess before the tidiness became a reality! Sometimes confusion is a necessary step toward clarity. It can mean that we are being shaken loose from the wrong thinking in which we have felt secure. But that may well produce a kind of mental uncertainty, even panic.

The problem is that we have misassembled the pieces of the puzzle, and the result is that we have gotten the picture wrong. It needs to be deconstructed. But now the pieces seem to be a jumble. We feel confused—until light dawns and the pieces begin to fit together properly. Only then can we see the picture clearly. Looking back, we realize that the confusion was a necessary stage in the clarification.

So, Jesus interrupts the disciples' conversations about their confusion in order to help them—just as a few days later He would do the same for two disciples on the Jerusalem–Emmaus road (Luke 24:13–35).

John allows us to eavesdrop on the conversation.

The disciples are asking, "What is this that he says to us, 'A little while, and you will not see me, and again a little while, and you will see me'; and 'because I am going to the Father'?"(John 16:17).

We know that "going to the Father" is Jesus' shorthand for His passion, death, burial, and resurrection, leading to His ascension to the right hand of God. Within a few hours, He will be dead and buried, and for "a little while" they will not see Him— in fact, they will feel they will never see Him again. But after "a little while," they will see Him again—when He is resurrected.

A leading British economist, asked one December to give his economic forecast, made the delightful comment that "the significance of Christmas will not become clear until Easter." He meant, of course, that it would take the economists some time to work out how profitable the Christmas season had been (and what the effects of borrowing for it would be!). It would probably be Easter-time before the picture was apparent. But like Caiaphas before him (John 11:49–52), he spoke deeper truth than he intended. This is exactly what Jesus has been telling His disciples—the meaning of His incarnation will become clear only in His resurrection. Christmas needs Easter if it is to make sense. Without the resurrection, the entire story ends in confusion.

Similarly here: the reason the disciples are confused is because they are trying to understand Jesus without taking into account His death and resurrection. Without the resurrection, His death will make no sense to them. A resurrection-less gospel is no gospel at all—as Paul emphasized (1 Cor. 15:12–19). The fears that arise because Jesus is leaving can only be resolved by the knowledge that He will return—in the resurrection.

From this principle, Jesus draws a realistic and important lesson—as His trademark emphasis indicates ("Amen, Amen," "Truly, truly"). He paints a word-picture:

"Truly, truly, I say to you, you will weep and lament,
but the world will rejoice.
You will be sorrowful,
but your sorrow will turn into joy.
When a woman is giving birth,
she has sorrow because her hour has come,

but when she has delivered the baby,
she no longer remembers the anguish,
for joy that a human being has been born into the world.
So also you have sorrow now,
but I will see you again,
and your hearts will rejoice,
and no one will take your joy from you."
(John 16:20–22)

What joy there is when the labor pains are over, and a child is born! So too, joy will follow the disciples' sorrow.

Jesus' illustration is intended to teach a yet deeper truth, a principle that governs all discipleship. The joy that a child has been born does not merely follow the pain of the labor; it is through the pain of the labor that the joy of the birth comes. True, the relationship between the disciples' pain and their coming joy will be chronological, but it will also be causal. The pain is productive of the joy. In the life of discipleship, there is a "joy that seekest me through pain."[1]

This is the consistent New Testament teaching about the relationship between tribulation and joy, suffering and glory. True, there is suffering now and there will be glory then. But, more than that, the glory is produced out of the raw materials of the suffering just as out of a woman's labor pains comes the joy of new life. For the Christian, there is purpose, and therefore meaning, even in the darkness. We may not understand the details of God's ways, but William Cowper (who knew much about the darkness) was right:

Deep in unfathomable mines
Of never-failing skill
He treasures up his bright designs,
And works his sov'reign will.

Ye fearful saints, fresh courage take;
The clouds ye so much dread
Are big with mercy, and shall break
In blessings on your head.[2]

"He plants his footsteps in the sea, and rides upon the storm," Cowper writes. He was echoing the Asaph-psalm:

Your way was through the sea,
     your path through the great waters;
     yet your footprints were unseen. (Ps. 77:19)

Like Cowper, Asaph seems to have had a streak of melancholy in his personality. He asks the hard questions about the presence of God in the dark. How can we see His way when He "plants his footsteps in the sea" where in the nature of the case they disappear immediately?

We would be naive Christians if we imagined we can always understand what God is doing or where He is going. But we have a Father who is working all things together for His children's good. Jesus is teaching His disciples that suffering becomes the raw materials in the Father's hands, and from it He means to create glory. Sorrow will lead to joy.

God is a potter; we are His living clay. Sometimes His molding and shaping of our lives hurts. But it has in view our transformation into the image of Christ. He is changing us "from one degree of glory to another" (2 Cor. 3:18). He is shaping something of lasting beauty. "This light momentary affliction is preparing for us an eternal weight of glory beyond all comparison." But if we are to see this, we must look in the right direction: "We look not to the things that are seen but to the things that are unseen. For the things that are seen are transient, but the things that are unseen are eternal" (4:17–18).

In our lives, the time gap between the suffering and the glory may be long. But on this occasion, Jesus reassures the disciples that they will experience this divine pattern in a little while. It will be illustrated in a period of only a few days—from a Friday afternoon through a Sunday morning. It may seem an eternity, but it will be only "a little while" until their time of tribulation gives place to a day of joy and glory: "You have sorrow now, but I will see you again, and your hearts will rejoice, and no one will take your joy from you" (John 16:22).

What will be true for Jesus Himself—"who for the joy that was set before him endured the cross, despising the shame" (Heb. 12:2)—will be true for the disciples. And these next few days in their lives will become the paradigm for all their days—and ours. Understanding this sustains disciples through their suffering.

We flinch from suffering. Christians are not masochists. Pressures can easily overwhelm us and sink us. But we see what is invisible—that the Father is always working to fulfill His purposes for us, in us, through us, and beyond us. He is forming in us individualized reflections of His glory. If so, we can be encouraged to yield to His molding of us, and learn to pray, "Father, this is sore; but please produce glory in me through it."

This paradigm was virtually the first lesson that Jesus taught His disciples after His resurrection. Remember what He said to the two on the Emmaus road? "Was it not necessary that the Christ should suffer these things and enter into his glory?" (Luke 24:26).

If this was true for the Master, then it will also be true—at least in miniature—for His disciples.

But Jesus has yet more to teach them about this pathway. Again, it is an important enough lesson to be prefaced by His trademark "Truly, truly": "In that day you will ask nothing of me. Truly, truly, I say to you, whatever you ask of the Father in my name, he will give it to you. Until now you have asked nothing in my name. Ask, and you will receive, that your joy may be full" (John 16:23–24).

The time is coming when they will see Him no longer—but it will be short, for they will see Him soon again. However, beyond that, a day is coming when they will never see Him again in this world. What then? What are they to do when they are no longer able to ask Him for counsel, wisdom, direction, or comfort?

Jesus' answer is to spell out for the disciples the wonderful privilege He is giving them: they can go to His Father! And when they go to Him, they can use Jesus' name!

The disciples had never before prayed: "Our Father, . . . we ask in Jesus' name." In fact, no one had ever prayed that way before. But this privilege is part of the inheritance He is leaving with them. They need not doubt that they will receive all the help they will need when they enter the presence of the Father and pray in the name of His Son!

In spelling this out, Jesus tells the disciples that He will no longer use "figures of speech": "I . . . will tell you plainly about the Father" (John 16:25).

Throughout His ministry, Jesus had employed figures of speech—He gave living water; He was the Bread of Life and the Light of the World. When speaking about their union with Him, He had used the extended metaphor of a vine and its branches. When speaking about their sufferings, He had used the metaphor of a mother in labor. But the time has come to speak without metaphors. Now, when He tells them about the Father, He is speaking "plainly."

The Father

There is a Father in heaven. At the heart of Jesus' ministry was His purpose to bring His disciples, His "friends," to know His Father as their Father too.

Old covenant believers did not call God "our Father" except in the sense that He was the Creator of the world and also the Creator of the nation of Israel. But now a new stage in divine revelation has been reached. Now that the Son has come, the Father can be known.

The God of the Old Testament is the same as the God of the New Testament. He does not change. But His revelation of Himself is progressive. John had already explained in the prologue to his gospel that it is only in the coming of the Son of God that we see Him clearly:

And the Word became flesh and dwelt among us, and we have seen his glory, glory as of the only Son from the Father, full of grace and truth. . . . For from his fullness we have all received, grace upon grace. For the law was given through Moses; grace and truth came through Jesus Christ. No one has ever seen God; the only God, who is at the Father's side, he has made him known. (John 1:14, 16–18)

Only now, when the Son is revealed, does it become clear that there is a "Father."

B.B. Warfield uses a helpful illustration:

The Old Testament may be likened to a chamber richly furnished but dimly lighted; the introduction of light brings into it nothing which was not in it before; but it brings out into clearer view much of what is in it but was only dimly or even not at all perceived before. . . . Thus the Old Testament revelation of God is not corrected by the fuller revelation which follows it, but only perfected, extended and enlarged.[3]

There are a few places in the Old Testament where God the Father "almost comes into view." Psalm 103:13 is an example: "As a father shows compassion to his children, so the LORD shows compassion to those who fear him." But almost from the moment we turn the blank page between the Old and the New Testament, an explosion of references hits us.

Leaf through the New Testament from the beginning. By the time you have reached page 5 or 6, you are reading the Sermon on the Mount with its frequent references to "your Father."[4] There are many more references to the Father in this one sermon than in the entire Old Testament! God was eternally Father, Son, and Holy Spirit. But only with the appearance of the Son on earth does this become clear. When the Apostles looked back, the knowledge of God possessed by the old covenant saints—wonderful as it was— seems like the experience of being taken to elementary school by a household servant in comparison with being grown up and able to enjoy your inheritance![5]

Now disciples call God "Abba, Father" (Rom. 8:15; Gal. 4:6).

In the Christian church, calling God "Father" is a commonplace. But it is worth pausing here to consider two important aspects of this. The first relates to our apologetics[6] and the second to our own spiritual health.

Apologetic Thinking

When Jesus speaks of the "Father," He is not using a metaphor. "Father" is not an anthropomorphism (a way of speaking about God in terms that belong properly to human beings). In fact, in one sense it is we who are using metaphorical language when we use the word *father* to speak about our human fathers. Our fatherhood is not the model for God the Father. The reverse is the case: His fatherhood is the model for ours. He is the original; we are the copy. In this sense, when we say "father," we are using a theomorphism (speaking about humans in terms of language that belongs originally to God).

This is an important principle to grasp, because it clarifies our thinking in the face of one of the most common "put-downs" of the Christian faith—namely, projectionism, the idea that faith in God the Father is merely a projection of a person's own needs.

The roots of this critique of the Christian faith are complex, but in popular culture we can trace it back to thinkers like Karl Marx (1818–83) and the Austrian psychiatrist Sigmund Freud (1856–1939): God the Father is simply a form of wish fulfillment. But this projectionism has deeper roots, going back into the philosophy of Ludwig Feuerbach (1804–72).[7]

But beyond this lies the European theology that virtually fed into the views of these thought leaders. Behind them lies the work of the theologian Friedrich Schleiermacher (1768–1834), who taught that the essence of true religion lies in a sense of ultimate dependence.

Schleiermacher was reacting to the European Enlightenment and especially the philosophy that denied the possibility of real objective knowledge of God—expressed, for example, in the thought of Immanuel Kant (1724–1804). Schleiermacher thought he was in fact saving Christianity from intellectuals he described as "cultured despisers of religion."[8] In essence, he argued that they had missed the point because they failed to understand that religion's real essence lay in the consciousness of the individual. Thus, those who denied the possibility of objective knowledge of God had missed the point!

In thinking that he could save the contents of his theological shop, Schleiermacher was in danger of giving it away. For if theology is based on our subjective consciousness, it is only one step away from this to say that it is a projection of our needs. Our sense of dependence on God as a heavenly Father, rather than indicating there is such a being, only indicates a sense of need that projects His existence. It is a short step from there to projecting the idea of God, and not too large a step from this to the conclusion that "religion is the opiate of the people"—a metaphor made famous by Karl Marx but widely used in the opium-interested world of the nineteenth century.

Since this is the atmosphere in which we find ourselves as Christians today, it is important for us not to read the Bible's language about God as Father through lenses crafted by a contemporary world-and-life-view. For biblical theology always works in the opposite direction. It begins with God. He "projects" Himself onto His creature man: "Then God said, 'Let us make man in our image, after our likeness. . . .' So God created man in his own image, in the image of God he created him; male and female he created them" (Gen. 1:26–27).

God is a Father to His children; they were therefore created to want and need Him as their Father. He helps us understand this by the very way He has created us. We are not modeling His fatherhood on ours, nor projecting our need. Rather, this "need" is the inevitable implication of our creation in His image. We "need" Him for exactly the same reason fish need water: that is how we were created.

Thus, God's fatherhood is the archetype (the original); ours is the ectype (the copy).

In other words, we are the projection!

So, what Jesus says here in the upper room wonderfully clarifies our thinking. He tells us we can go to the Father. He is not using metaphors, similes, or any other figure of speech. There is a Father. And He should know—for, after all, He is the Son!

But this revelation of God as Father is also important pastorally.

Pastoral Medicine

Our Lord's emphasis on knowing God as our Father reappears in the first conversation He has after His resurrection. He thus underlines its importance when He says to Mary: "Go to my brothers and say to them, 'I am ascending to my Father and your Father, to my God and your God'" (John 20:17)

The Lord Jesus is simply confirming and applying the truth He had taught in the upper room. The disciples have come to know and love the Son of God as their Savior and Lord. They can, therefore, be reassured that "the Father himself loves you" (16:27). Now, like Jesus, they can call Him "Abba, Father."

None of them had been taught by their parents to pray, "Our heavenly Father . . ." But now that the Son has revealed Him, they can go directly to the Father themselves. All they have to do is use Jesus' name, and they will discover—as Jesus now says—"The Father himself loves you" (16:27).

If you were looking for wording to inscribe in a card to a Christian friend—no matter what their situation—could you find better words? They contain powerful pastoral medicine.

Throughout the centuries, the great masters of the spiritual life have observed that many Christians suffer from a sinister syndrome—a deep-seated and damaging suspicion of God the Father. Since it can lurk deep within the psyche, it is important to be able to recognize its symptoms and to apply gospel medicine to it.

It manifests itself in different ways.

You may be sure that the Son loves you, yet, somehow or another, have less confidence that the Father really does.

Or, and perhaps this is more common, you may think that the Father loves you only because Jesus died for you.

Sometimes, sadly, the way the gospel is preached subtly communicates this latter message to us.

For example, a preacher may say: "You are sinful. But here is the good news of the gospel: God loves you because Christ died for you."

We need to think through the implications of that statement, because in effect it turns the gospel on its head.

This becomes obvious if we reflect on the words of John 3:16: "For God so loved the world, that he gave his only Son, that whoever believes in him should not perish but have eternal life." John's syntax makes clear that in referring to "God," he means the Father—since He "gave his only Son." He is therefore saying virtually the reverse of: "God (the Father) loves you because Christ died for you." Rather, he is saying that the real truth is: "It is because God (the Father) loves you that the Son died for you."

A mere theological technicality? Hardly, since misspeaking the gospel is never a mere technicality. And in this case, the logical implication of the way it is presented is that the Son persuaded the Father to love you. And this in turn injects into us a deepdown feeling that we may never quite recognize or articulate to ourselves: we can trust the love of the Lord Jesus unreservedly, but we cannot be quite so sure of the Father. How can we be if He loves us only because Jesus did something to persuade Him?

So long as that is the case, this sinister syndrome will be present. It may lie dormant, it may have periods of remission, but it will always be there, ready to emerge in the harmful symptoms of doubt, anxiety, weak faith, and a lack of assurance and joy.

But here is the medicine that cures: Jesus said, "I and the Father are one" (10:30); "Whoever has seen me has seen the Father" (14:9). And here is a theological elixir that heals when taken daily: "The Father himself loves you" (16:27).

When you have seen Jesus' love for you, you have seen the Father's love. You have seen everything there is to see!

Here is how one of these spiritual masters of a past generation expressed it. John Owen's centuries-old words are worth reading slowly and pondering thoughtfully:

> How, then, is this love of the Father to be received so as to hold fellowship with him? I answer, By faith. The receiving of it is the believing of it. God hath so fully, so eminently revealed his love, that it may be received by faith. . . .
>
> It is true there is not an immediate acting of faith upon the Father, but by the Son. . . .
>
> Jesus Christ, in respect of the love of the Father, is but the beam, the stream; wherein though actually all our light, our refreshment lies, yet by him we are led to that fountain, the sun of eternal love itself. Would believers exercise themselves herein, they would find it a matter of no small spiritual improvement in their walking with God.
>
> This is that which is aimed at. Many dark and disturbing thoughts are apt to arise in this thing. Few can carry up their hearts and minds to this height by faith, as to rest their souls in the love of the Father; they live below it, in the troublesome region of hopes and fears, storms and clouds.

All here is serene and quiet. But how to attain to this pitch they know not. This is the will of God, that he may always be eyed as benign, kind, tender, loving, and unchangeable therein; and that peculiarly as the Father, as the great fountain and spring of all gracious communications and fruits of love.

This is that which Christ came to reveal: God as a Father.[9]

Unacquaintedness with our mercies, our privileges is our sin, as well as our trouble. . . . This makes us go heavily, when we might rejoice, and to be weak, where we might be strong in the Lord. How few of the saints are experimentally acquainted with this privilege of holding immediate communion with the Father in love! With what anxious, doubtful thoughts do they look upon him! What fears, what questionings are there, of his goodwill and kindness! At the best, many think there is no sweetness at all in him towards us, but what is purchased at the high price of the blood of Jesus. It is true, that alone is the way of communication; but the free fountain and spring of all is in the bosom of the Father.[10]

If this touches a nerve in us, we need to fix our minds on these words of Jesus and let them flood our hearts: The Father Himself loves you.

Here is something to say to ourselves every day. They are simple words, but life-changing, peace-giving, poise-creating. If the coming of the Spirit persuades the disciples of this, then it will shed a flood of light on why Jesus is leaving them and going to the Father (16:28). But we have been talking together outside the upper room for a few minutes. We must return to it.

Perhaps now, knowing all that the Spirit will do when He comes to them, the disciples will realize that it is to their "advantage" that Jesus is leaving them. He is going to ask the Father to keep His promises to Him. He will then send His own Spirit to them. When He comes, they will be able to say—as Paul later does—that "God's love has been poured into our hearts through the Holy Spirit who has been given to us" (Rom. 5:5). They will know that the Father loves them. And they will be secure.

The response of the disciples seems encouraging: "His disciples said, 'Ah, now you are speaking plainly and not using figurative speech! Now we know that you know all things and do not need anyone to question you; this is why we believe that you came from God'" (John 16:29–30).

Their mood has changed! There is a new confidence. But this was not the first time Jesus had witnessed a reaction of: "We've got it now; and we'll never lose it." So, He reminds them again that trials still lie ahead of them: "Do you now believe? . . . You will be scattered . . ." (John 16:31–32).

Yet their trials will be small by comparison with His. They "will be scattered, each to his own home" (v. 32). But Jesus, by contrast, will experience His trial "alone" (v. 32). Yet He will not ultimately be "alone." The Father who loves them also loves Him and will be with Him.

Here then is His final explanation of why He has spent this time with them. We have seen that the word He spoke cleansed them; it was also intended to bring joy; and now He adds: "I have said these things to you, that in me you may have peace. In the world you will have tribulation. But take heart; I have overcome the world" (v. 33).

As Jesus concludes His direct teaching, He gives the disciples two promises.

The first is peace (Hebrew *shalom*). In Christ, there is *shalom*. Through His work, there will be peace with God; by the Spirit's ministry, there will be restoration.

The second is victory. He has "overcome the world." In Christ, there is triumph; they will become more than conquerors through Him (Rom. 8:37).

We have come to the end of four chapters in which we have been listening to the Savior talking to His disciples and showing them how He loves them "to the end" (John 13:1). Now, in the final chapter, we will hear Him pray—the eternal Son speaking to His Father. It is one of the most sacred moments recorded in all Scripture. As the disciples followed Him into this Holy of Holies, they did so with His words echoing in their ears: "When you trust in Me, you will have peace in the midst of this world's disquiet, and you will experience victory over all the enemies of the gospel."

It is our privilege to follow them.

11

—

The Heart of Christ Opened

John 17:1–5

When Jesus had spoken these words, he lifted up his eyes to heaven, and said, "Father, the hour has come; glorify your Son that the Son may glorify you, since you have given him authority over all flesh, to give eternal life to all whom you have given him. And this is eternal life, that they know you, the only true God, and Jesus Christ whom you have sent. I glorified you on earth, having accomplished the work that you gave me to do. And now, Father, glorify me in your own presence with the glory that I had with you before the world existed."

How do you get to know someone well? You talk with them face-to-face. But sometimes we get to know them even better if we overhear them talking face-to-face with the person they love most. The ease of relationship, the freedom to speak from the heart, the knowledge that there is no danger of misunderstanding, the lack of fear in sharing secrets—all make for a freedom of expression, a keeping of nothing back.

The same is true of our knowledge of the Lord Jesus Christ. In these chapters, we get to know Him better as we overhear Him speaking to His "friends." But we get to know Him best of all in this chapter because in it we overhear Him speaking to His heavenly Father. John knew that. And so, in this section of his gospel, he includes not only the actions, conversations, and teaching of Jesus (in chs. 13–16), but also His prayer (ch. 17).

This is, truly, "the Lord's Prayer." It is the longest prayer in the New Testament.

Earlier, the disciples had been full of questions. Almost half of them—Simon Peter, John, Thomas, Philip, and Judas—had all asked them. But they have all fallen silent (16:5). Only Jesus' voice has been heard. And now He is no longer addressing them. Instead, He allows them to overhear Him speaking to His heavenly Father.

In some ways, chapters 13–17 are a gospel within the gospel; in fact, they reflect the shape of the whole.

The book begins with a prologue and ends with an epilogue.

In between there are two volumes—the Book of Signs and the Book of Glory.

Similarly, these chapters begin with a prologue—Jesus washing His disciples' feet.

In between there are two sections. In chapters 13 and 14, Jesus speaks to the disciples about His departure and promises that He will send the Spirit to be with them.

THE HEART OF CHRIST OPENED

Then, in chapters 15 and 16, He urges them to abide in Him and promises them that He will keep them through their coming tribulation.

The section then ends with an epilogue—Jesus prays for Himself and then for His disciples.

From the time of the Reformation, this chapter has been known as Christ's "High Priestly Prayer." John does not specifically describe Jesus here as a high priest, and so some scholars avoid using that description. Nevertheless, the prayer follows a pattern that governed the ministry of the high priest on the annual Day of Atonement.

The Day of Atonement

Under the old covenant, sacrifices were offered daily, first in the tabernacle and later in the Jerusalem temple. Teams of priests served in rotation throughout the year.

The tabernacle and the temple shared a basic ground plan. There was a courtyard, beyond which were two rooms: the Holy Place and the Most Holy Place or the Holy of Holies (i.e., the holiest room).

Sacrifices were offered every day in the Holy Place. But once a year, on the tenth day of Tishri, the seventh month in the Jewish calendar (our September or October), the high priest went into the Holy of Holies. This was where the ark of the covenant was kept, and it was regarded as the throne room of God on earth. It was the sacred space into which the high priest came to present the annual sacrifice for the sins of the people and to pray for them.

This was a holy occasion. No one else in Israel was permitted to enter the Most Holy Place. The high priest himself was allowed access only once in the year.

The regulations for the Day of Atonement were spelled out in Leviticus 16:1–34. The high priest would sacrifice a young bull for his own sins and those of the priests and sprinkle its blood on the mercy seat of the ark and on the ground in front of it.

In addition, he would take two goats and cast lots over them to determine the specific functions of each.

He would kill one goat and sprinkle its blood over the mercy seat as a sin offering.

He then took the second goat, placed his hands on its head, and confessed the sins of the people. This goat was then taken out into the desert and released, symbolically carrying away the sins of all Israel into the wasteland. The first goat was "for the LORD" and dealt symbolically with the guilt of the people. But the second goat was "for Azazel" (Lev. 16:8–10). This came to be known, via the King James translation, as "the scapegoat"—a word we are familiar with as meaning "someone who takes the blame that really belongs to others."[1]

By the time of Jesus, the high priest's preparation for his ministry on the Day of Atonement was carefully structured. He cleansed himself by ritual washing; he engaged in an all-night vigil. Several men were appointed to help him stay awake through these hours of prayer. We can hardly avoid thinking here of Jesus' self-consecration (John 17:19) and of His words to the disciples in the garden of Gethsemane: "Are you asleep? Could you not watch one hour? Watch and pray" (Mark 14:37–38; the verb for "watch" means "stay awake").

The high priest's intercession was formed of three concentric circles: first, he prayed for himself and the ministry that he was about to exercise; then he made intercession for those who were consecrated with him to the Lord's service; and third, he prayed for all the people of God.

This symbolism is now coming to fulfillment in the Lord Jesus, the High Priest of the new covenant. The true and final Day of Atonement is dawning. Soon the shadows of the old covenant will give way to the reality—but not by the offering of the blood of a bull and goat or by a sin-bearing goat being led out into the wilderness. These sacrifices needed to be repeated year after year. As the New Testament makes clear, old covenant believers would have been able to work out that such repetition meant that they had no power to take away their guilt permanently or deliver them from spiritual bondage effectively. No, God was only "covering over" sin until the time when a single sacrifice would be made to take it away permanently. As Paul notes, "In his divine forbearance he had passed over former sins" (Rom. 3:25). But now, as the true and final High Priest, Jesus is about to make a sacrifice that will take away sin and bring deliverance from bondage once and for all: He will offer Himself, and His own blood; He will carry our guilt away fully and finally and overcome the evil one.

Against this background, Jesus follows the high priestly pattern:

17:1–5:   He prays for Himself and His ministry.

17:6–19:   He prays for His immediate disciples, the men His Father had given Him to share with Him during His public ministry.

17:20–26:   He prays for all who will become Christian believers ("I do not ask for these only, but also for those who will believe in me through their word").

This includes us. By whatever means it has reached us, it is through the word of the Apostles, now enshrined in the pages of the New Testament, that we have come to believe in Him.

The scope of our Lord's prayer is breathtaking! It includes His own ministry during the hours now unfolding, it encompasses the ministry of the Apostles in the next generation, and then His intercession reaches forward as far as the church today as He catches us up in His prayer and brings us to His Father.

These, then, are sacred moments in John's gospel. In a sense, they take us back to its opening words. For here Jesus is *pros ton theon*, face-to-face with God, and *eis ton kolpon*, "at the Father's side" (1:1, 18). This whole chapter is like a stethoscope through which we can hear the Savior's heartbeat.

These are also moments of deep emotion. Only here does Jesus address God as "Holy Father" and "O righteous Father." Having "emptied himself, by taking the form of a servant," He must now be "obedient to the point of death, even death on a cross" (Phil. 2:7–8).

Jesus Prays for Himself

Now, finally, "the hour has come" (John 17:1). Twice before, in the context of a meal (the wedding at Cana) and a feast (of Booths), Jesus had said that His hour or time had not come (2:4; 7:6). But now, at this last supper, He knows it has arrived. The Greeks who had asked to see Him earlier in the week had been a signal to Him (12:20–21). Here in the upper room, He had sensed that the devil was mounting his final attack (John 13:2, 27). All the players were in position. The Scriptures were about to be fulfilled. These included the promise of the Psalms that one of His own companions would betray Him. But now the most ancient of all promises was on the verge of fulfillment. The hour had come when His heel would be crushed, but under it He was about to crush the serpent's head.

So how does Jesus pray for Himself, and for what? Does He pray that there might be some other way? No, not yet—although in another hour or so, the coming God-forsakenness of the cross will make Him long that there might be an alternative ("My Father, if it be possible, let this cup pass from me," Matt. 26:39).

Does He then pray for strength? In truth, He needs it and will soon enough pray "with loud cries and tears, to him who was able to save him from death" (Heb. 5:7). He will be heard, and an angel will come to strengthen Him (Luke 22:43). But that prayer is still an hour or two away. His present burden is different: "When Jesus had spoken these words, he lifted up his eyes to heaven, and said, 'Father, the hour has come; glorify your Son that the Son may glorify you'" (John 17:1).

"Father, . . . glorify your Son." There is no other prayer in history quite like this. True, in one sense it is legitimate for every believer to reflect the words of Paul and pray, "Father, You have promised to transform me 'from one degree of glory to another' (see 2 Cor. 3:18). Please work that glory into me." But this is different, because the glory in view is "the glory that I had with you before the world existed" (John 17:5). This is not "reflected glory"; Jesus calls this "my glory" (v. 24).

Several features of this petition stand out.

The Deity of the Son

Jesus' words are a powerful expression of His self-consciousness, His awareness of His eternal identity. He knows who He is— the Son of God—and therefore glory is His by right. He is the One who was at God's side and face-to-face with Him from all eternity (John 1:1, 18). He knew that He had come from God and was going to God and that the Father had given all things into His hands (13:3). This is not the language of a mere man.

Our Lord was intimately familiar with the Old Testament Scriptures. He knew Yahweh's words, "My glory I will not give to another" (Isa. 48:11). Yes, later that evening He would preface His prayer in a different way: "Father, if it be possible, let this cup pass from me. . . ," but not here. He does not pray, "Father, if it is possible, will You glorify Me?" Rather, He asks directly for what is His by right as God's Son, and which, in addition, His Father has promised to give Him.

Jesus is the Son of the Father. He therefore always—in eternity as well as time—conforms to the commandment to "honor your father." In His humanity, our Lord expressed this honor by obedience. He is the Eternal Father's *pais* ("child," "son," or "servant"; Acts 3:13, 26).[2] He is a child going to His Father and saying, "Father, You promised; please will You keep Your promise now?"

But Jesus is also the eternal Son, "of one substance, power, and eternity" with the Father. The glory of God ("the glory I had with you before the world existed") is His by right as well as by promise.[3]

But what is this "glory"?

Glory

In Scripture, the glory of God is the external expression or manifestation of His being and His invisible attributes and perfections. It is revealed in the kaleidoscopic bursts of the eternal magnificence of God's being and character displayed in the created order (Pss. 19:1–6; 29:1–11; Rom. 1:19–23). By such means God "speaks," as it were, declaring: "You cannot see Me because I am the invisible God. But I clothe Myself in these magnificent garments to give you a sense of how majestic and glorious I really am."

Psalm 29 dramatically illustrates this. It describes the people of God experiencing a thunderstorm—apparently when they have gathered for a worship service: lightning flashes across the sky; thunder crashes through the atmosphere; there is a supernaturally planned fireworks display of the majesty and power of God. God's people respond instinctively: "In his temple all cry, 'Glory!'" (Ps. 29:9).

John had already seen Christ's glory at the wedding in Cana (John 2:11). The Synoptic Gospels tell us that he saw it again on the Mount of Transfiguration (Luke 9:32). He saw it once more on the island of Patmos in a vision. But in the incarnation, the Son had not only "emptied" Himself but had also "veiled" His glory. But now His "hour" has come. It is the "hour" of His shame. But it is also time for Him to return to His Father. His deepest desire is for the veil to be removed so that it will be evident that He is "the radiance of the glory of God and the exact imprint of his nature [as the One who] upholds the universe by the word of his power" (Heb. 1:3).

When we are asked, "Does the New Testament teach that

Jesus was God?" we often refer to texts like John 1:1 and Romans 9:5. But here, in John 17, we find Jesus expressing His own sense of His deity. Glory is His, and also "authority over all flesh, to give eternal life to all whom you have given him" (v. 2). Only One who is Himself God can claim glory for Himself; and none other than God Himself has authority to give eternal life to sinners!

This consciousness of His own deity is further underlined by Jesus' definition of the eternal life that He has unique authority to give. It is to "know you, the only true God, and Jesus Christ whom you have sent" (v. 3). Only if the Son is "God with God" has He any right to mention knowing Himself and knowing God in the same breath!⁴

But Jesus' words also underline that His being glorified and our being blessed belong together. Our coming to know Him with His Father and experiencing eternal life is one of the ways the Father will glorify His Son!

His Glory, Our Blessing

People often assume that the glory of God stands in antithesis to their own blessing and may even be His calculated denial of it. It is as if they believe—as they in fact do—that every ounce of glory God gets proportionately diminishes their happiness and pleasure. And who in his right mind would want to glorify God under those circumstances?

But that is the problem. Scripture tells us that when it comes to spiritual realities, by nature we are not in our right mind: "They became futile in their thinking, and their foolish hearts were darkened. Claiming to be wise, they became fools, and exchanged the glory of the immortal God for images" (Rom. 1:21–23).

The result is that what was known by children in the remote regions of eighteenth-century Scotland, or in many places in the young United States, is a complete mystery to the most sophisticated and academically qualified unbeliever: "Man's chief end is to glorify God, and to enjoy him forever."[5]

God's glory and our enjoyment go hand in hand! But in sharp contrast, "All have sinned and fall short of the glory of God" (Rom. 3:23). We have broken God's law, and therein lies our rebellion. But what Paul's words underline is the tragedy of our situation—we have fallen short of the glory of God. We have lost our way and forfeited the destiny for which we were made. And that in turn means we have also lost the enjoyment of God. No joy, no glory.

The Path to Restoration

How we will be restored to this is embedded in Jesus' prayer. The "hour has come" for Him to complete the work of restoration. He came to glorify the Father. For Him to do that, the Father must glorify the Son. How does this double glorifying take place? The answer becomes clearer if we follow Jesus' thinking here.

It will help us do this if we understand that the logic of His thinking is not identical with the order of His speaking. That is often the case in Scripture because it is often the case in our conversation in general. Perhaps the best way to unfold the logic is by means of a short catechism based on John 17:1–5.

When does Christ pray? When "the hour has come" for the Father to glorify the Son so that the Son may glorify the Father (v. 1).

How does the Lord Jesus glorify His Father? "I glorified you on earth, having accomplished the work that you gave me to do" (v. 4).

What was this "work"? "To give eternal life to all whom you have given him" (v. 2).

What is this eternal life? "And this is eternal life, that they know you, the only true God, and Jesus Christ whom you have sent" (v. 3).

How does the Lord Jesus accomplish it? "You have given him authority over all flesh" (v. 2).

When will Jesus accomplish this work? "I . . . accomplished the work that you gave me to do" (v. 4).

How does the Father glorify the Son? ". . . in your own presence with the glory that I had with you before the world existed" (v. 5).

We noted earlier that the pattern in the prologue to the whole gospel is given dramatic form in the prologue to this section of the gospel: the Word, the Son, belongs to the world of glory but steps into the world of shame to bring us to the glory to which He returns. This same pattern is present now in the "prologue" to our Lord's prayer. He has come from the glory He had with the Father before creation. He came to rescue His people from eternal death and give them eternal life before returning to His Father and sharing heaven's glory.

Since this is the climax of the promise God gave in Genesis 3:15, we should pause here to notice that in the background lies the very beginning of the Bible's storyline.

God created man in His image, to reflect His glory. He made a garden for him to care for (Gen. 2:8, 15). This garden expressed the glory of God, which is why there are echoes of it in the tabernacle and later in the "garden-city-world" of the new Jerusalem (Rev. 21–22). But while all creation was "very good" (Gen. 1:31), it was not yet all garden. Adam—and presumably his family line with him—was to extend this garden and populate it until it reached "the ends of the earth." To accomplish this task, they were given "authority over all flesh" (John 17:2; see Gen. 1:28). Scripture gives us hints that when this was accomplished, Adam, with all his family, would then bring this garden-city-world back to God as the love-gift of their obedience, and say, "I glorified you on earth, having accomplished the work that you gave me to do" (John 17:4).

This was a truly wonderful calling with a glorious destiny. But Adam failed and fell. Instead of exercising authority over the earth from which he had been created, he became part of it in the disintegration of death: dust he was, and to dust he returned (Gen. 3:19). He forfeited forever the eternal life for which he had been created—life lived in the presence of God, in communion with God, in the enjoyment of God.

Only when we see the glorious privileges for which we were originally created can we sense the tragedy of the present human condition: "All have sinned and fall short of the glory of God" (Rom. 3:23).

But now the die is cast for our restoration. The Lord Jesus has reached a stage in His ministry in which His death, resurrection, and ascension are settled. There is no turning back.

So, what is this "work" the Father gave Him to do in order to give us eternal life? We can answer that question best if we understand His "work" within its full redemptive-historical context.

The "Work"

Jesus is the "last Adam" and "the second man" (1 Cor. 15:45, 47). He came to undo what Adam did and to do what Adam failed to do. Thus, He became the High Priest of creation that Adam and his posterity were called to be but failed to become. Soon He will have done everything necessary to begin His work of restoration. Now the authority on earth that the first man, Adam, lost will be regained by the second man and last Adam, Jesus Christ (1 Cor. 15:22–28, 45–49).

This is why the Lord Jesus is now able to say what Adam never could: "I glorified you on earth, having accomplished the work that you gave me to do" (John 17:4). In less than twenty-four hours, He will say, "*Tetelestai*—it is finished." Having completed the work Adam failed to do, Jesus then did what Adam refused to do: He "bowed his head" (19:30). On "Good Friday," He took the judgment Adam deserved for his sin and crushed the head of the serpent who had become the ruler of this world.

So, what we are overhearing in Jesus' prayer has its roots in the opening three chapters of Genesis. And this may make you wonder if there is special significance in the note John will later interject into his account of Mary Magdalene's Easter Sunday morning encounter with the risen Lord: "Supposing him to be the gardener . . ." (John 20:15).

Yes, Mary must have been confused. She did not recognize Jesus until He spoke in His all-too-familiar accent. And yet, perhaps John sees more clarity than confusion here. For Jesus is the gardener Adam failed to be. And He means to extend that resurrection garden to the ends of the earth through the preaching of the gospel (Matt. 28:18–20) and into the lives of all the Father has given Him (John 17:2).

It is in this way that the Father will glorify the Son, even as the Son glorified the Father.

The Joy of the Son

Jesus' prayer about His own glory is also about His joy. The author of Hebrews tells us that it was because of "the joy that was set before him" that He "endured the cross, despising the shame" (Heb. 12:2).

This is not to say that our Savior's earthly pilgrimage was joyless. Far from it. He is specifically said to have "rejoiced in the Holy Spirit" (Luke 10:21). But in a world that was unsuited to His perfect holiness, He could never be totally "at home" or "settle down." He must have felt that He belonged not to its sinful culture but to the holy air of the heavenly land. Perhaps the nearest we ever get to it is experiencing homesickness.

The Welsh have a specific word for this: *hiraeth*. The *Oxford English Dictionary* defines it as "deep longing for a person or thing which is absent or lost; yearning; nostalgia."[6]

We are too familiar with sin to be sensitive to its deep perversity. We have breathed in its atmosphere so long that we have lost the ability to taste or smell its pollution. We think of it as normal. So, we rarely wonder at the Son of God's willingness to come "in the likeness of men" (Phil. 2:7) and breathe the same air we do. We are too desensitized by familiarity to be able to imagine what it must have been like for Him.

Perhaps an allegory will help.

The Stranger in Smokeland

The Stranger had lived all his life in the Highlands. Here streams of crystal-clear water run; the flowers and vegetation are luxuriant; the mountain air is pure; the atmosphere is unpolluted. No one who lives here has ever died.

But the Stranger's father had told him of a distant land where the air is polluted, and the inhabitants die young. The pollution and death are caused by a plant the citizens roll into tube-shapes, light, and place in their mouths, and then they inhale its vapors—they do not realize they are poisonous. Instead, they find their highest pleasure in this; they believe it keeps them healthy and that it protects them and is essential to a good life.

The parliament of the country has never enacted a law to this effect, but it is universally regarded as unacceptable for a citizen not to smoke. Now they have become so addicted to the lighted plant that they can no longer smell the odor it leaves on their bodies, their hair, and their clothes. They think that its effect on their skin and eyes enhances their attractiveness.

The Stranger and his father feel pity for this land. They decide that the Stranger should visit it, instruct its people, offer to rid the land of its pollution, and make a treaty for them that will guarantee clean air, good health, and endless life.

And so, the Stranger comes to Smokeland.

The citizens see that the Stranger never smokes. This makes them feel uncomfortable. He begins to talk to them about a land where no one smokes, where the air is fresh, the rivers are crystal clear, and everyone is healthy. He tells them that in this kingdom no one has ever died. He also tells them that his father, who reigns over the land from which he has come, sent him to Smokeland to set its citizens free from smoking and to rid their land of its noxious atmosphere. The air, he promises, will become pure, their breath will become clean, their clothes will no longer be impregnated with the odor of the plant—they will feel like new people altogether!

But instead of admiring his obvious health and listening to his message, the citizens of Smokeland become angry. They refuse to believe the Stranger; they tell him his claims cannot be true. They deny that they are unhealthy; they enjoy the smell of their clothes; they reject his message.

Nevertheless, despite the mounting opposition to him the Stranger continues to speak. He pleads with them to listen. But this simply angers the people. Now they plan to silence him.

One day they surround him, exhaling their smoke, breathing it over him. "Smoke! Smoke! Smoke like us!" they chant.

He refuses, but they insist. And when he still will not smoke, they surround him in even greater numbers. They press in on him, jeering, blowing the smoke of the lighted plant onto his face and into his eyes. They try to push the lighted tubes of it into his mouth. But he refuses to inhale. They persist. His clothes are now reeking from their polluted smoke, his face is surrounded by their exhaling, and he is covered in their spittle. His eyes are watering, and his heart is longing for relief and for the fresh air of home. But he refuses to smoke.

At last, the Smokeland citizens' anger flares up into mob-rage at the Stranger's persistence. Some of them seize him and hold him while others begin to stab at his body with their lighted tubes of the noxious plant. Finally, one of them pours flammable liquid over the Stranger's head. They take the small flares they use to light the plant, and set his clothes ablaze. He is burned to ashes before them . . . he has endured the intolerable smoke to the end without yielding to the Smokers. They do not realize that he will rise again, phoenix-like, from the ashes.

The allegory needs little interpretation. Our Lord was loved and glorified from all eternity by holy angels and archangels, by sacred cherubim and seraphim. He lived in the enjoyment of the pure atmosphere of the mutual love of the Father and the Spirit. What, then, must it have been like for Him to become the Stranger, the One who "endured from sinners such hostility against himself" (Heb. 12:3)? What must it have been like, emotionally, for His sinless soul, deeply sensitive to the pollution in the atmosphere that surrounded Him, to live among us, and then for our intolerance of His holiness to lead to His crucifixion?

If Lot was "greatly distressed by the sensual conduct of the wicked" and was "tormenting his righteous soul over their lawless deeds" (2 Peter 2:7–8), do you not think that our Lord must have felt a deep *hiraeth*?

He rarely gives expression to it. But He did so, perhaps significantly, on His descent from the Mount of Transfiguration, where He had for a while breathed the pure atmosphere of heaven: "O faithless and twisted generation, how long am I to be with you? How long am I to bear with you?" (Matt. 17:17).

There must have been times when Jesus longed to be home

in the glory that He had with the Father before the world began. The prospect of it sustained Him through the shame.

So, behold Him as He prays. He is coming to His heavenly Father—"Father, you know My *hiraeth*, the homesickness that has been My life these long years. But throughout them all, I have glorified You! And now the darkest hour has come. But through it, I am coming to You: glorify Me in Your own presence with the glory I had with You before the world began."

It is a privilege beyond words to be allowed to overhear these words.

Perhaps we can imagine that the Father was thinking:

"My Son, I have watched You every single day. I know the atmosphere into which I sent You has been almost unbearable to Your holy soul. But You have been faithful to Your calling to be 'a high priest, holy, innocent, unstained, separated from sinners,' and You will be once again 'exalted above the heavens' (Heb. 7:26).

"Now that You have washed Your disciples' feet and will soon wash away their sins by the shedding of Your blood, it will not be long until You resume Your place of honor at My right hand.

"I will highly exalt You, as I have promised, and give You the name that is above every name. And at Your name, My Son, every knee will bow—in heaven and on earth and under the earth— and every tongue will confess that You are Lord.

"You will be glorified with the glory You had with Me before the world began."

In these few verses, we are given the privilege of overhearing the Son, the second person of the Trinity, telling His Father, the first person of the Trinity, what He most wants in all the world and desires for all eternity.

We know that the Father always hears Him (John 11:42).

Now His prayer has been answered. He is glorified; countless knees bow to Him; countless tongues confess that He is Lord.

Many years ago now, as I got into a hotel elevator at the start of a conference at which I was speaking, the bellboy—it was a nice hotel!—nodded in the direction of the reception desk. I looked over to see who else was checking in for the conference. The young man asked me, "Is that Dr. Everett Koop?" (the former surgeon general of the United States, and well known for his Christian faith).[7] "Yes," I replied. "He must be coming to the conference." I was thrilled to see that he would be present. But the bellboy said something that also thrilled me. He turned to me as he closed the elevator door and said, "He's the one who saved me from smoking!"

It was a great moment. And it was a miniature picture of the day when countless millions will look at Jesus Christ and say, "He's the One who saved me!"

Surely this makes you love the Lord Jesus when you think of all that He endured for you?

Surely it makes you rejoice that His Father has glorified Him?

Surely, since His Father has done that, you should do it too?

12

The Father's Gift

John 17:6–19

"I have manifested your name to the people whom you gave me out of the world. Yours they were, and you gave them to me, and they have kept your word. Now they know that everything that you have given me is from you. For I have given them the words that you gave me, and they have received them and have come to know in truth that I came from you; and they have believed that you sent me. I am praying for them. I am not praying for the world but for those whom you have given me, for they are yours. All mine are yours, and yours are mine, and I am glorified in them. And I am no longer in the world, but they are in the world, and I am coming to you. Holy Father, keep them in your name, which you have given me, that they may be one, even as we are one. While I was with them, I kept them in your name, which you have given me. I have guarded them, and not one of them has been lost except the son of destruction, that the Scripture might be fulfilled.

But now I am coming to you, and these things I speak in the world, that they may have my joy fulfilled in themselves. I have given them your word, and the world has hated them because they are not of the world, just as I am not of the world. I do not ask that you take them out of the world, but that you keep them from the evil one. They are not of the world, just as I am not of the world. Sanctify them in the truth; your word is truth. As you sent me into the world, so I have sent them into the world. And for their sake I consecrate myself, that they also may be sanctified in truth."

"The disciple Jesus loved" knew why the atmosphere in the room had changed when Judas left. But was he now wondering where he had gone, and what he was doing? So far, Jesus has "lost" none of His disciples—except Judas, "the son of destruction"—but what will happen to the rest of them? What did Jesus mean when He said that all the disciples would be scattered?

And then there is Peter. Was he embarrassed by his response to the foot-washing? If so, that must have paled into insignificance by comparison with the Master telling him that he would have denied Him three times before the next day had fully dawned (John 13:38). Surely Jesus was mistaken?

But now all the disciples are silent because Jesus is praying—and they have never heard Him pray quite like this before.

The prayers of Jesus recorded in the Gospels are marked by great simplicity. But this prayer was different. In it, He was praying for Himself—just as the high priest did on the Day of Atonement. Yes, its language was still simple—they could easily follow what He was saying. But what He was praying about took them out of their depth—the glory of God—and He spoke of this glory as His glory!

But now there is a change of gear. Having prayed about Himself, Jesus now prays for His colleagues—just as the high priest did—for these eleven men who have been with Him throughout His ministry. They are His "friends," His spiritual family.

This is the longest section of the prayer (it takes up more than half the chapter).

Jesus had so many requests to make for these men—yet, while His focus on them begins in John 17:6, He does not actually ask anything for them until halfway through verse 11. The first part of His prayer is a description of them, not intercession for them!

The Father's Gift

The disciples are the Father's love-gift to His Son. Although He describes them in this way in other sections of His prayer (17:2, 24), there is an intensity here—He repeats the description again and again:

v. 6: "I have manifested your name to the people whom you gave me out of the world."

v. 6: "Yours they were, and you gave them to me."

v. 9: "I am not praying for the world but for those whom you have given me."

v. 11: "Keep them in your name, which you have given me."

Imagine a young Christian man who has fallen in love with a girl in his college. He is praying about their relationship. How does he speak to God about her? He will probably begin by describing her: "Lord, she is so beautiful, and I love everything about her; and she loves You, Lord. . . . It is amazing to me that You have brought us together. Lord, I pray . . ."

The young man is not naive. He does not think that God needs to be told any of these details. He is simply opening his heart to God and telling Him why this girl is so important to him.

There is a deep instinct in love that makes it include descriptions of loved ones in intercession for them. So here, Jesus is telling His Father why these disciples matter so much to Him. Perhaps in these moments of heightened emotion, He also wants them to overhear the language He used when He prayed for them privately. It is His favorite way of describing these eleven men— not as "disciples" or "Apostles" or even as "friends." They are all that, but supremely they are the men whom the Father has given Him (John 6:39).

Jesus loves the disciples as they are, warts and all—although He has no intention of letting them remain in that condition! But what touches Him most deeply is that they belonged to His Father and are His love-gift to His Son. Their chief worth is found not in themselves but in the fact that the Father has loved them. And now, in essence, He has said, "My Son, I love these men so much that I am giving them to You in order for You to save them."

This, of course, was the plan of the Trinity. With one mind and will, the Father, the Son, and the Holy Spirit envisaged the salvation of these men.

This salvation required their election by the Father—since

those who are rebels against God will not first choose to trust and love Him.

It also required the sacrifice of the incarnate Son—because the guilty cannot atone for their own sins.

It then required the work of the Holy Spirit to bring about their new birth and faith in Christ—because the spiritually dead cannot resurrect themselves.

The Father, the Son, and the Spirit—the triune Lord—planned all this in eternity. But now, as this plan is being effected in time, the disciples have the privilege of overhearing the incarnate Son speaking to His Father about them.

Did His description of them take their breath away? Did they think then, or only later: "Is this who I really am? Is this what He meant a moment ago when He said, 'The Father himself loves you' (16:27)? Lord, this is amazing love! I am the love-gift Your Father has given You!"

At this point, Jesus is praying for His immediate disciples only (17:9). But the rest of the New Testament makes clear that every disciple has been given to the Son by the Father (Eph. 1:4; 1 Peter 1:2). We are of eternal value to the Lord Jesus. Not because of our inherent worth—for we have none now—but because we are the Father's love-gift to Him. By means of this gift, the Father shows how much He loves us. By means of this description, Jesus shows how much He loves His disciples. By means of this prayer, the disciples discovered that each one of them could describe himself as "the disciple whom Jesus loved" (John 21:20).

When we begin to trust in Christ as these men did, we too can say about ourselves, "I am the disciple whom Jesus loved." For:

The love of Jesus, what it is
None but his loved ones know.[1]

Chains of Grace

Various "chains" or connecting links bind the Father to the Son
and the Son to the Father and then the disciples to the Father
and the Son. For example, the Father loves the Son, and the Son
loves the disciples. Again, the Father sends the Son, and the Son
sends the disciples.

But there are two "chains" that stand out in Jesus' prayer.

The Chain of Glory

The first is "the chain of glory." The Father is the Father of an infinite
glory. The Son comes to glorify His Father. The Father responds by
giving glory to the Son (John 17:1–5). In turn, the Son will be glorified in the disciples (v. 10). Indeed, the glory the Father has given
to the Son He in turn gives to all His disciples (v. 22). And His
ultimate desire for them is that they will see Him in the glory that
the Father gave Him before the foundation of the world (v. 24).
All this will be accomplished by the Holy Spirit, the other Helper
Jesus is going to send to them from the Father: "When the Spirit
of truth comes, . . . he will glorify me, for he will take what is mine
and declare it to you. All that the Father has is mine; therefore I said
that he will take what is mine and declare it to you" (16:13–15).

But how, exactly, will the Spirit "declare" it? The answer is
found in a second "chain"—the chain of the Word of God.

The Chain of the Word

Jesus had indicated that part of the Apostles' Spirit-enabled
function would be to give the church what we call the New

Testament—containing the record of Jesus' teaching, the interpretation of that teaching, and the significance of His future activity. The Spirit would remind them of Jesus' teaching and help them understand its implications. As a result, they would be enabled to author the Gospels and the other books of the New Testament (John 14:26). He would lead them into the truth about Christ during the days covered by the Acts of the Apostles, and enable them to expound "the truth [as it] is in Jesus" in the Letters (John 16:13; Eph. 4:21). And He would show them what was still to come (in the book of Revelation, as well as in parts of the Letters).

But now, in His prayer, Jesus puts this in a larger context:

He speaks about:	The words the Father gave the Son (17:8)
These are:	The words the Son has given to the Apostles (v. 8)
This is:	The word the Apostles have received (v. 8)
In turn, this is:	The word the Apostles have kept (v. 6)

As a result, they have come to know who Christ is. They have also come to believe in Him as the Son sent by the Father (v. 8). And as a result, the world has hated them (v. 14).

| So, Jesus prays that: | The word they received will sanctify them (v. 17) |
| And also prays about: | The word they preach so that others will believe (v. 20) |

There is a remarkable parallel between the "glory-chain" and this "word-chain":

Glory belongs to the Father;
> Glory is given to the Son;
>> Glory is given by the Son to the Apostles;
>>> Glory is seen through the Apostles' ministry
by
>>>> all disciples.

And this happens because:

The word belongs to the Father;
> The word was given to the Son;
>> The word was given by the Son to the Apostles;
>>> The word was given through the Apostles
to
>>>> all disciples.

When we discuss the authority of the New Testament, we often turn to the "big texts," such as 2 Timothy 3:16–17. But in some ways, what Jesus is saying here in the upper room is even more fundamental: the Word we have received from the Apostles was given to them by the Son through the ministry of the Holy Spirit. And the words of Christ were sourced, in turn, by the Father Almighty!

This is why we can trust the Apostolic Word. It is through these Spirit-breathed, Spirit-illumined, Spirit-applied Scriptures that we are kept, sanctified, and ultimately glorified. It is when we read them "with unveiled face, beholding the glory of the Lord," that we are "transformed into the same image from one degree of glory to another." And while the Lord Jesus does not mention it in His prayer it is already clear from His teaching in these chapters that "this comes from the Lord who is the Spirit" (2 Cor. 3:18).

This is what the New Testament is for. And this is the ultimate goal in our study of John 13–17. So, let us immerse ourselves in the Word of God so that we will emerge reflecting a little more clearly and fully the glory of the Lord!

Preservation and Sanctification

John's gospel records a drama in which the Son of God comes from glory so that those who have fallen short of God's glory might behold it in the face of Jesus Christ and come to reflect it in their own lives.

Now, in these "epilogue" moments in the upper room, Jesus is praying that this will be true for His disciples. But if it is to happen, they will need to be both preserved and sanctified. So He prays "keep them" and "sanctify them" (John 17:11, 17).

Preservation

The disciples will arrive at their destination only if they are guarded throughout the whole course of their journey. As Peter would later put it, this required not only that their inheritance be kept for them but also that they should be kept for their inheritance (1 Peter 1:4–5). Was he, perhaps, transposing the prayer he had heard in the upper room into teaching for Christians under pressure as he had once been?

Until now, Jesus had been with them. He had kept and guarded them Himself (John 17:12). If they were anything like us—which they were—they probably hardly ever noticed His protection. True, they had needed it during the storm on the Sea of Galilee and perhaps on a few other occasions. But Simon Peter had sometimes reversed the roles in his imagination and seen himself as Jesus' protector. As recently as an hour or so earlier, he had confidently predicted he would lay down his life to protect his Master (13:37). And an hour or so later, he would actually attempt to be Jesus' protector, slashing the ear of a servant of the high priest (18:10–11). How little he knew about his frailty. He was the one who needed to be guarded and protected. So, Jesus brings him and the others to His Father: "They are so fragile, Father. But until now I have been with them, in front of them, protecting them; around them, guarding them. None of them has been lost—only Judas, who was never truly one of them. But I am leaving this world—and leaving them in it without My visible presence. They cannot survive on their own. Father, keep them, and keep them united so that their fellowship will be a powerful testimony to the gospel and others will come to believe in Me."

What does Jesus ask His Father to do for them in order to keep them? He specifically does not ask that they should be taken out of the world (17:15). Rather, He prays, "Sanctify them in the truth; your word is truth" (v. 17).

Sanctification

What does this mean? We are given a clue: a moment later Jesus says that He had sanctified or consecrated Himself for them (17:19).

In the New Testament, "to sanctify" can be used of gradual, ongoing purification, but it usually refers to a once-for-all radical and decisive act in which God reserves us for Himself.

You need a new couch for your living room. You have seen one advertised that looks perfect. But when you arrive at the store, the couch has a sticker on it that says "reserved." Someone else came into the store earlier and bought it. You cannot have it. It is being kept for them, even though they have not yet taken it home. So—hands off!

This is what Jesus is praying about. He is asking His Father to protect the disciples by setting them apart for Himself. He places His "reserved" sticker on us. We are His now. We are kept for Him.

But by what means will the disciples be sanctified? The answer may seem paradoxical. They will be sanctified by the very thing that will put them at risk in the first place. They will be persecuted because they keep the word the Father gave to His Son to give to them and then to pass on to others (John 17:8, 20). But that same word will protect them; it will keep them "reserved for God." So, Jesus prays, "Sanctify them in the truth" (v. 17).

Martin Luther experienced this paradox once his conscience was captured by the Word of God. The very Word for which he was persecuted was the Word by which he was protected! So, he could sing from experience:

And though this world, with devils filled,
Should threaten to undo us,
We will not fear, for God hath willed
His truth to triumph through us.
The Prince of Darkness grim,
We tremble not for him;
His rage we can endure,

For lo! his doom is sure;
One little word shall fell him.

That word above all earthly pow'rs—
No thanks to them—abideth;
The Spirit and the gifts are ours
Through him who with us sideth.
Let goods and kindred go,
This mortal life also:
The body they may kill:
God's truth abideth still;
His kingdom is forever.[2]

Jesus is praying here that the Word of God will keep His disciples from the hostile world into which He is sending them (John 17:11, 13–14), from the power of the flesh to weaken and divide them (v. 11), and also from the wiles of the devil, who will seek to destroy them (v. 15).

Our Lord is praying not to be "seen by others" but to be heard by His Father in heaven (Matt. 6:5–6). Nevertheless, He tells His Father why, on this occasion, He wants to be overheard by others. He wants His disciples to know His deepest desires for them: "These things I speak in the world, that they may have my joy fulfilled in themselves" (John 17:13).

This echoes what He had told them earlier. His word would bring them joy in a world of stresses and sorrows (15:11). He wanted them to know what He was praying for them, and that, as they found themselves "pruned" by opposition, His word would dwell in them richly (cf. 15:3, 7, 10). Through it they would be kept—protected by God and reserved exclusively for Him. Jesus' ministry did not end in the upper room. He is now at the right hand of God interceding for His people. He is in the presence of His Father on their behalf, living forever in heaven to make intercession for them (Rom. 8:34; Heb. 7:25; 9:24). What we have in John 17, as older writers used to say, is a transcript of His present intercession for the whole church.

What a privilege for the Apostles to listen to these words and hear the intimate thoughts of their Master.

What a privilege for them to know how much they meant to the Son of God.

What a privilege for them to learn that the Father had given them in love to His Son.

What a privilege for them to overhear Him praying that they would be protected.

And what a privilege for us to eavesdrop on these words so that we too can hear the heartbeat of our Savior.

That privilege is about to increase. There is more to come. For now we will overhear the Savior praying specifically for us.

13

He Prays for Me

John 17:20–26

*unity
relationship* [handwritten]

"I do not ask for these only, but also for those who will believe in me through their word, that they may all be one, just as you, Father, are in me, and I in you, that they also may be in us, so that the world may believe that you have sent me. The glory that you have given me I have given to them, that they may be one even as we are one, I in them and you in me, that they may become perfectly one, so that the world may know that you sent me and loved them even as you loved me. Father, I desire that they also, whom you have given me, may be with me where I am, to see my glory that you have given me because you loved me before the foundation of the world. O righteous Father, even though the world does not know you, I know you, and these know that you have sent me. I made known to them your name, and I will continue to make it known, that the love with which you have loved me may be in them, and I in them."

D o you ever come to the end of a book of the Bible, or perhaps hearing (or even preaching) a series of sermons on
it, and feel you have only been scraping the surface? There is so
much more. Now you feel you are only ready to begin studying it!

It would not be surprising if we felt the same way as we come
to the closing verses of John's description of events in the upper
room on the evening before Jesus' crucifixion. So, these pages can
only be a beginning. But now they bring us to the words with
which Jesus' prayer ends—John 17:20–26.

The Lutheran theologian David Chytraeus (1530–1600)
seems to have been the first writer to describe this chapter as Jesus'
High Priestly Prayer. Whether or not John thought of it that way,
we have noticed that its shape reflects three stages in the ministry
of the Jewish high priest as he prepared for the sacrifices to be made
on the Day of Atonement. He interceded for himself, then for his
colleagues in the priestly family, and then finally for all Israel.

In the same way, Jesus prays for Himself—the road ahead is a
Via Dolorosa to Gethsemane and Calvary and the Garden Tomb.
But beyond that is glory.

He then prays for His immediate colleagues and family—the
now eleven Apostles who have been with Him "from the beginning" (John 15:27). They are being sent out into the world with
His word; they need His Father's protection. Jesus is praying that
they will be sanctified through the word the Father gave Him,
which He in turn has given to them.

But as we come to the closing verses of the chapter, we are
greeted by the unexpected. Jesus' prayer extends far beyond the
horizon of His own lifetime. He now prays "for those who will
believe in me through their [the Apostles'] word" (17:20).

This prayer was answered in the events recorded in the Acts of the Apostles and the New Testament Letters. But its focus is more expansive than that. In these words, Jesus was also praying for me if I am a believer. For we, too, are among those who have come to believe in Christ through the Word of the Apostles (v. 20).

In addition, since this prayer is a transcript of the heart of Christ on the evening of His passion, it is also an indication of His will for us after His resurrection and ascension. Since He prayed in this way for us then, we also discover here what He desires for us now. In a sense, therefore, His intercession not only encourages and secures us; it teaches us how to live in conformity with our Savior's will.

Here, then, are words to turn to frequently to remind ourselves what Christ most wants.

What Jesus Wants

He prays for our unity. "I do not ask for these only [i.e., the Apostles], but also for those who will believe in me through their word [which includes us], that they may all be one, just as you, Father, are in me, and I in you, that they also may be in us, so that the world may believe that you have sent me" (John 17:20–21).

Jesus was not thinking here of a grand worldwide organizational unity. It is not organization but spiritual vitality that makes the church able to withstand the gates of Hades (Matt. 16:18). The kind of unity Jesus envisages is patterned after the personal, mutual indwelling of the Father and the Son ("as you, Father, are in me, and I in you," John 17:21).[1] Just as the Father and Son live together in the fellowship of the Spirit, so, since every believer is indwelt by that same Spirit, our fellowship begins to mirror Theirs.

There is nothing in the world like this unity. It cannot be imitated in clubs, in sports teams, or in the esprit de corps of a school. Relationships in these contexts are natural, rooted in a common interest or commitment. But the unity of disciples is supernatural, patterned after the very being of God. And it is created by the indwelling of one and the same Holy Spirit in each member of the fellowship.

Paul saw the implication of this when he wrote to the Colossians about the nature of the church family: "Here there is not Greek and Jew, circumcised and uncircumcised, barbarian, Scythian, slave, free" (Col. 3:11).

There were still Greeks and Jews, slaves, and freemen in the first-century church. Paul's point is not that the gospel creates an organized uniformity but that because "Christ is all, and in all," the fellowship of Christians transcends all natural and social distinctions and divisions. When Christ is all to us and we recognize that He indwells each of us by His Spirit, a bond of fellowship and love is created that is unparalleled in the world. The reason is simple: those who experience it are not "of the world" (John 17:16). It is therefore not possible for the world to fabricate an imitation!

What lies behind this prayer is the teaching Jesus had already given the disciples. It would take some time for them to process, as it does for us. But it transforms our entire perspective on each other: this brother, this sister in Christ is someone into whose life the Father and Son have come. Christ indwells him or her through His Spirit. That is why, although we retain our diversity of nationality, skin color, age, education, social background, and much else, we are one in Christ. The result is that the "differences" only serve to highlight the beauty of the unity of grace that prevails.

Why did Jesus think this so important? We could guess, but He does not leave us to speculation. This Spirit-given unity in a church family is essential for our evangelism—if only we would see it. He is praying that we may be one: "so that the world may believe that you have sent me . . . , that they [disciples] may become perfectly one, so that the world may know that you sent me and loved them even as you loved me" (John 17:21, 23).

Our Lord's burden is that His church will be His chief evangelistic agency and that the fellowship Christians have with each other will make a powerful evangelistic impact.

There is an important corrective inherent in this prayer. During the last two centuries or so, much, perhaps most, of the literature, the seminars, and the emphases in evangelism have stressed the priority of "personal witness." In addition, many Christians associate "evangelism" with organizations that have little or no connection to the church.

Two problems inevitably arise when this is the case.

The first, and perhaps most obvious, is that even if someone comes to faith in Christ, there is still a gap between them and the life of a church fellowship. Conversion and fellowship in the church tend to remain two different things. But clearly in the way Jesus' prayer was first answered—on the day of Pentecost—coming to Christ and becoming part of the church family were two sides of the same coin (Acts 2:41–47).

The second problem is one for which our churches are probably as much to blame as parachurch evangelistic organizations. Each of us is always to be "prepared to make a defense to anyone who asks you for a reason for the hope that is in you" (1 Peter 3:15). But in the New Testament, evangelism is not seen as a dominantly individualistic activity. In view in our Lord's prayer here is that the church family, not the isolated individual, is God's chief evangelistic instrument. It is the sphere in which the effect of the gospel is most fully reflected and the transformation salvation creates is put on display.

Understanding this is particularly significant in our contemporary culture of individualism, fragmentation, and alienation—a world in which the truth and lifestyle of the gospel have both been rejected. It is in the fellowship of the church family that non-Christians will most powerfully encounter the kingdom of God and the "new creation" (2 Cor. 5:17).

You may have heard testimonies like this: a young woman opposed to the gospel and its lifestyle finds herself—very reluctantly—in a gathering of the church family of someone she knows. She hates everything she thinks these people believe. But she finds herself confronted by a question: "How is it that I believe these people stand for everything I hate, and yet when I am with them and watching I feel that this is the way life was meant to be lived? I see it in their relationships with each other, in the harmony of the atmosphere, in the children and their parents, and in the young people's relationships with the elderly. How is it that they seem to possess the very things I lack? Why do I ache inside for what they have?"

Of course! In a world where sin has deconstructed the foundations on which life was meant to be built, people encounter an entirely new world in a living church family. Yes, it is imperfect, but it is a world where life approximates to what God meant it to be.

It is also the answer to Jesus' prayer, ". . . that they may all be one, . . . so that the world may believe that you have sent me . . . and loved them even as you loved me" (John 17:21, 23).

No wonder Jesus prays for our unity.

Before we consider what follows, notice a detail that we can easily pass over without much thought. Jesus explains the cause of this unity: "The glory that you have given me I have given to them, that they may be one even as we are one" (v. 22).

Christ creates a new fellowship. Its analogy is His mutually indwelling relationship with the Father. Its goal is that the world should come to believe in Him. Its cause is His giving to His disciples the glory that His Father first gave to Him.

What can this mean? How is this possible when we know that God will not give His glory to another (Isa. 48:11)?

Here again we encounter what Paul calls "the depths of God" (1 Cor. 2:10). We should, therefore, tread reverently. It will help us to do that if we see how the teaching John records builds up to this point:

1. Jesus had already given clues to His meaning by speaking about His fellowship with the Father (John 10:30; 14:11). He is one with Him, not by any identity of persons[2] but in personal union (17:11; cf. vv. 8, 22).
2. The Father indwells the Son, and the Son in turn indwells the Father (1:1, 18; 14:10–11; 17:23). They therefore have all things in common—except the personal distinctions appropriate to fatherhood and sonship.[3]
3. The Father and Son, therefore, possess, share, and communicate the same glory.

4. Since during the incarnation the Son remains "face-to-face" with God and is still "at the Father's side" (1:18), this mutual indwelling continues.
5. This being the case, the mutual communication of glory continues. Thus, the glory the Father gave His Son manifests itself in His humanity (1:14; 2:11; 12:28; 17:1, 4, 5).
6. Through the coming of the Spirit, the Father and the Son, who mutually indwell one another, will now indwell believers and make Their home with them (14:23).
7. Since this is so, the glory that has been manifested in the humanity of the Lord Jesus will also be manifested in those who are united to Him.
8. In this way, the glory the Father has given to the Son in the unity-in-personal-diversity will come to expression in the glory of the unity-in-personal diversity of the fellowship of believers.

In very simple terms, what Jesus is praying for is that when people encounter the church, they will see many different pieces of a puzzle fitting together and revealing His own face. Thus, when our Lord's prayer, offered for the church in every age, is answered in our local church family, the glory of Christ will become visible. The result will be an inbuilt evangelistic attraction in our worship and fellowship. This in turn will arrest the attention of unbelievers and draw them to Christ.

Since this is the case, it should not surprise us if our churches become targets of Satan.

We noted earlier from the Acts of the Apostles that when the devil's strategy of intimidation of the church failed, he shifted to a second tactic of stirring up ambition in the church, in the false motivations and actions of Ananias and Sapphira (Acts 5:1–10). But our Lord's prayer in John 17 was answered for the Jerusalem church—they were kept by God's power, and they were sanctified by the Word. As a result, something significant took place:

1. Acts 5:11:   And great fear came upon the whole church . . .

2. Acts 5:13:   None of the rest dared join them, but the people held them in high esteem.

3. Acts 5:14:   And more than ever believers were added to the Lord, multitudes of both men and women.

This is a different pattern from the one that became de rigueur in much late-twentieth and early twenty-first-century speaking and writing about evangelism. There, "seeker sensitivity" dominated. Here, Jesus' prayer was answered by the sense of awe that was present in the church. The pattern of Acts was:

1. The holiness of the church;
2. The awe of God among His people;
3. A complex response from non-Christians—not daring to join because sinners are conflicted by the holiness of God's people as they are kept by the Word and committed to it;
4. The floodgates open and there are conversions.

If this was how Christ's prayer for His church was answered then, do you not think that it must illustrate His heart's desire for our churches today?

This brings us to our Lord's final words.

What Jesus Wants for Us

If we have been treading on holy ground in these chapters in John's gospel, we come in 17:24 to the holiest place of all.

Listen to what Jesus prays for us: "Father, I desire that they also [i.e., those who would come to faith through the Apostles' word, v. 20], whom you have given me [this includes Christians today], may be with me where I am, to see my glory that you have given me because you loved me before the foundation of the world" (John 17:24).

Notice the main verb—"I desire [*thelō*, I want, I will] . . ."

An hour or so later, in Gethsemane, Jesus will pray in a radically different way: "Father, if it be possible, let this cup pass from me; nevertheless, not as I will . . ." (Matt. 26:39; Matthew uses the same verb, *thelō*).

These two prayers are so different, but they are intimately connected.

Jesus is able to pray as He does in the upper room ("I will . . .") only because of what He will pray in the garden ("not as I will . . ."). He was willing to drink the cup of God's judgment when every instinct in Him shrank from the prospect of the God-forsakenness of Calvary. That made it possible for Him to say here, "I will that those You have given Me may be with Me . . . to see My glory . . . and not only in the occasional glimpses they have seen here, but in a manner that expresses Your eternal love for Me!"

Facing the great crisis of His life, Jesus was thinking about us. His will is that we should see Him in His glory. This is why Paul is so confident: "When Christ who is your life appears, then you also will appear with him in glory" (Col. 3:4). He has prayed that it will be so.

But why is it so important to Jesus that we should see Him in His glory?

The words that follow give us a clue: "O righteous Father, even though the world does not know you, I know you, and these know that you have sent me" (John 17:25).

The world had rejected His Father and continued to do so. It had also rejected Him. The disciples have been at His side now for three years, watching Him at close quarters. They are about to witness His final rejection. We too have witnessed this rejection continuing down through the years, into our own lifetime and even into our own lives.

Jesus wants those who have been witnesses of His shame to see Him in His glory!

In the summer of 1987, the feathers of the All England Lawn Tennis and Croquet Club were ruffled by the winner of the Wimbledon men's singles title (one of the four tennis majors). The Australian victor, Pat Cash, instead of meekly waiting for the presentation of the trophy from a member of the British royalty, daringly climbed up through the stands to greet his father and the team that had supported him. Apparently, the chairman of Wimbledon told him to enjoy the moment but promise never to do it again—he had kept members of the royal family waiting!

Pat Cash later commented on his derring-do (repeated by others, despite the chairman!): "That's what it was all about . . .

this team. They were really important to me." They had been with him when there were no crowds applauding, through the relentless hours of preparation, through the bad days as well as this great day. In a sense, he was saying, "I want to be with them and them to be with me now, to see my glory."

Even from a human point of view, we can understand that Jesus wants no less. So, He prays:

"Holy Father, I bring to You these eleven men who have been with Me all the way.

"I alone will gain the victory. But You gave them to Me, to be with Me and to be sent out with Your word. They are My friends.

"They will see Me despised and rejected, a man of sorrows, acquainted with grief, experiencing the shame of the cross—beaten, humiliated, stripped, and exposed. Some of them will witness My sense of dereliction at Calvary.

"And, Father, there are others who will come to trust Me because of the ministry of these men. They too will see My name demeaned; many of them will suffer for My sake and the gospel's. I am praying for them also.

"Holy Father, I want them all to see Me in My glory; I want them to see the wonder of Your eternal love for Me; I want them to be with Me, with Us—forever."

Yes, we too have seen the Lord Jesus demeaned. We too have heard Him being despised. We too have felt the pain of being associated with Him. In our weakness, we too have felt overwhelmed. Remember, then, that He has prayed for us too: "Father, I desire that they also, whom you have given me, may be with me where I am, to see my glory that you have given me because you loved me before the foundation of the world" (John 17:24).

And if you too are among those the Father gave to His Son, remember these things:

Remember that just as He prayed for Peter, He has prayed for you.

Remember that the Father always hears His prayers—not least this prayer for you.

Remember that He has made known His Father's name to you and brought you into His family.

Remember that He loves you with the love His Father has for Him.

Remember that the beloved Son of the Father dwells in you through His Holy Spirit.

Remember that He has given you His Word.

Remember that He has made known His will—He wants you to be with Him to see His glory.

And all this is recorded so that His joy might be in you and your joy might be full.

It was to bring this to pass for us that He prayed: "O righteous Father, even though the world does not know you, I know you, and these know that you have sent me. I made known to them your name, and I will continue to make it known, that the love with which you have loved me may be in them, and I in them" (John 17:25–26).

Notes

Introduction

1 Thomas Goodwin, *The Heart of Christ in Heaven towards Sinners on Earth* (London, 1651), in *The Works of Thomas Goodwin* (Edinburgh, Scotland: James Nicholl, 1862), 4:96.

Chapter 1

1 John tells us that Jesus did many miracles or signs. But in the first part of his gospel he specifically describes seven. These are: (1) turning water into wine, 2:1–11; (2) the healing of an official's son, 4:46–54; (3) the healing of a lame man, 5:1–15; (4) the feeding of the five thousand, 6:1–15; (5) walking on the sea, 6:16–21; (6) giving sight to a man born blind, 9:1–41; (7) the raising of Lazarus, 11:1–44.

2 John Calvin, *Commentary on the Gospel according to John*, trans. William Pringle (Edinburgh, Scotland: Calvin Translation Society, 1848), 21. Emphasis added.

3 For example, Jeremiah 32:1–15; Ezekiel 4:1–5:17.

4 The words are from the hymn "And Can It Be," written by Charles Wesley (1707–88) shortly after his conversion in 1738.

5 Westminster Confession of Faith 13.1 states, "They who are . . . regenerated, having a new heart and a new spirit created in them, are further sanctified really and personally, through the virtue of Christ's death and resurrection, by his word and Spirit dwelling in them."

Chapter 2

1 Cf. John 21:25.

2 The allusion is to the words "Be of sin the double cure, cleanse me from its guilt and power" from the hymn "Rock of Ages, Cleft for Me" by A.M. Toplady (1740–78).

3 While some Christians have taken Jesus' words literally, there is no indication in the New Testament to suggest the Apostles thought He was

instituting a third sacrament alongside baptism and the Lord's Supper. The New Testament indicates that these were continued in the church, and explains their significance. The only reference to foot-washing is in connection with the register of widows about which Paul speaks (1 Tim. 5:10: those enrolled must have "washed the feet of the saints"). But if this had been an ordinance in which the whole church literally participated, it could not have served as something that *distinguished* some widows from others. Like John (and Peter), Paul sees the action of our Lord in washing His disciples' feet as a model for Christian service.

4 Heidelberg Catechism 1.

5 The words of the Collect for Peace in the Book of Common Prayer of the Church of England.

6 From the hymn "Make Me a Captive, Lord" by George Matheson (1842–1906).

7 Paul employs this metaphor when he describes himself as following in the "triumphal procession" of Christ. Christ "spreads the fragrance of the knowledge of him everywhere. For we are the aroma of Christ to God among those who are being saved and among those who are perishing, to one a fragrance from death to death, to the other a fragrance from life to life" (2 Cor. 2:14–16).

Chapter 3

1 Jesus is the Light of men, coming into the world, shining in the darkness as the true Light (John 1:4–9); Nicodemus comes to Him "by night" (3:2); but men love darkness and hate the light and therefore do not come to it, unlike those who do what is true (3:19–20). Jesus is also the Light of the World, and those who follow Him do not walk in darkness (8:12), as He demonstrates in giving sight to a man born blind (9:5). But the night comes (9:4), and if people walk in it they stumble (11:10).

2 The reference in the title of Dalí's painting is not to the Apostle John but to the sixteenth-century Spanish Roman Catholic mystic John of the Cross (1542–91). An associate of Teresa of Ávila (1515–82), he was named in 1926 to the select company of theologians known as "Doctors of the Church."

3 The language of Mark 14:33 suggests Jesus felt as though His whole being was disintegrating under the mental, spiritual, and physical burden He was bearing: Jesus "began to be greatly distressed and troubled." This is the language Paul uses in Philippians 2:26 to describe the distress of Epaphro-

ditus. J.B. Lightfoot suggested the word describes "the confused, restless, half distracted state which is produced by physical derangement or mental distress, such as grief and shame and disappointment." J.B. Lightfoot, *Commentary on Paul's Epistle to the Philippians* (London: Macmillan, 1913), 123.

4   Two members of the Apostolic band were named "Judas." They are distinguished as (1) Judas Iscariot and (2) Judas the son of James (Luke 6:16), who may also have been known as Thaddaeus (Matt. 10:3; Mark 3:18) and who asks Jesus a question in John 14:22.

5   From the hymn "Rock of Ages, Cleft for Me" by A.M. Toplady (1740–78).

Chapter 4

1   The Roman historian Suetonius (69–130/140) attributed the words *iacta alea est* (the die is cast) to Julius Caesar when he crossed the River Rubicon in January 49 BC in defiance of the Roman Senate and initiated the civil war with Pompey (*De vita Caesarum*, 1.32).

2   From the hymn "And Can It Be" by Charles Wesley (1707–88).

3   From the hymn "My Jesus, I Love Thee" by William R. Featherston (1848–75). In sharp contrast to the modern accusation that penal substitutionary atonement is a form of "child abuse," John's gospel teaches us that it was the united purpose of the Father and the Son and that at no time during our Lord's life or death did the Father cease to love Him.

4   Psalm 24:7–10, Scottish Metrical Version. The psalm is usually sung to the tune "St. George's Edinburgh."

5   Tertullian, *Apology*, 39.

6   Augustine, *Confessions*, 10.33: "O Lord, hear me; look on me, see me, pity me, and heal me—You in whose sight I have become a puzzle to myself—which is my weakness."

Chapter 5

1   The Ten Commandments (Ex. 20:1–17; Deut. 5:1–21) were essentially the life principles God had written into the instincts of Adam and Eve when He created them as His image (Gen. 1:26–28). While not completely eradicated by sin (Rom. 2:14–15 seems to point to this), at Sinai they were rewritten on tablets of stone and given specific application to the children of Israel (1) as sinners, (2) as delivered from Egypt, and (3) as the nation from whom the promised Seed of the woman, the Messiah, would come. In the new covenant, it is these original creation laws (rather than the tempo-

rary civil and ceremonial applications of them in the Mosaic covenant) that are written on the hearts of believers (Jer. 31:33; cf. Heb. 8:8–13; 10:16).

2 The Vulgate translation reads in full: *ego sum via et veritas et vita. Nemo venit ad Patrem nisi per me.* In all likelihood, many of the first students were also familiar with the famous words of Thomas à Kempis: "Follow thou me. 'I AM the Way, the Truth, and the Life.' Without the Way, there is no going; without the Truth, there is no knowing; without the Life, there is no living. I AM the Way which thou oughtest to follow; the Truth which thou oughtest to trust; the Life which thou oughtest to hope for. I AM the Way inviolable, the Truth infallible, the endless Life." Thomas à Kempis, *Of the Imitation of Christ* (London: Griffith, Farron, Okeden & Welsh, 1886), 204.

3 Paul indicates by the way he asks these questions that he expects a negative answer. To express in English the way Paul asks his question (in Greek), we need to add words and say something like: "Not everyone works miracles, do they? Not everyone possesses gifts of healing, do they?"

4 To "ask anything" in Christ's name implies that the "anything" conforms to the Word and promise of God.

5 In the nature of the case, the role of an Apostle in the sense of these men, plus Matthias (Acts 1:21–22, 26) and Paul (1 Cor. 9:1), was an unrepeatable office in the church. Being an eyewitness of the risen Christ was an essential qualification because the office was foundational (Eph. 2:20). Extraordinary signs confirmed their ministries (2 Cor. 12:12; Heb. 2:4). This explains why, although instruction was given in the New Testament for the continuation of the roles of elders and deacons, in the nature of the case none was given for the Apostles.

6 If Jesus' words are to be understood to refer to all Christians, then, again in the light of Paul's words in 1 Corinthians 12:30, in view must be not His miracles as such but the effect of His ministry—namely, people coming to faith.

Chapter 6

1 John's language in his first letter is reminiscent of John 1:1: Jesus is the Word who was "with God [*pros ton theon*—face-to-face with God]"; He is now our "*paraklētos* with the Father [*pros ton patera*—face-to-face with the Father]" (1 John 2:1).

2 One of a number of statements made by Jesus in the upper room that clearly imply His awareness of His own deity—here in the way He associates Himself with God the Father.

3   This is the other Judas in the disciple band who was probably also known as Thaddaeus.

4   C.S. Lewis, *Mere Christianity* (1952; repr., William Collins, 1955), 170–71. As with much else in his works, Lewis acknowledges George MacDonald as the source of the idea here.

5   Augustine, *Confessions*, 11.14.

Chapter 7

1   *Middoth* 3.8, translated by Alfred Edersheim in *Sketches of Jewish Social Life* (London: Religious Tract Society, 1876), 304. It is also mentioned by the Roman author Tacitus in his *Histories*, 5.5, and by Josephus in *The Wars of the Jews*, 5.5.4, who notes that the grape clusters hanging on the golden vine were as tall as a man.

2   B.F. Westcott, *The Gospel according to John* (1881; repr., Grand Rapids, Mich.: Eerdmans, 1951), 217.

3   Despite my best efforts, I have been unable to locate the source of this quotation.

Chapter 8

1   A.N. Whitehead, *Process and Reality* (New York: Free Press, 1978), 39.

2   "Diabolos Meaning," Our Baby Namer, accessed June 23, 2020, http://www.ourbabynamer.com/meaning-of-Diabolos.html.

3   Such expressions and their equivalents are found in the writings of the early fathers in the first few centuries. *The Epistle to Diognetus*, 1; Clement of Alexandria, *Stromateis*, 6.5.39.

4   The expression is from the fifth-century Latin hymn *Te Deum laudamus*.

5   John Bunyan, *The Pilgrim's Progress*, ed. Roger Sharrock (Harmondsworth, England: Penguin, 1965), 211–12. The words are from the song of the shepherd boy whom Christiana (the pilgrim's wife) and the other pilgrims hear singing in the Valley of Humiliation. He is "in very mean clothes, but of a fresh and well-favoured countenance." Mr. Great-Heart says: "Do you hear him? I will dare to say, that this boy lives a merrier life, and wears more of that herb called hearts-ease in his bosom, than he that is clad in silk and velvet."

6   The title of chapter 13 of C.S. Lewis, *The Lion, the Witch, and the Wardrobe* (London: Geoffrey Bles, 1950, and many other editions).

Chapter 9

1   The word *apostle* (Greek *apostolos*) means "someone sent/commissioned/a messenger." It is used in the New Testament some eighty times and in

basically four contexts: (1) of messengers in general (John 13:16), (2) of Jesus as the One sent by His Father (Heb. 3:1), (3) of people sent by their churches on a mission (2 Cor. 8:23), and (4) of "the Twelve" plus Paul, who serve as eyewitnesses of the risen Christ and who have been commissioned by Christ, with a ministry related to the whole church. The men who were now listening to Jesus in the upper room belonged to this fourth category.

Chapter 10

1 From the hymn "O Love That Wilt Not Let Me Go" by George Matheson (1842–1906), the pastor-hymnwriter who lost his sight in his youth.

2 From the hymn "God Moves in a Mysterious Way" by William Cowper (1731–1800).

3 B.B. Warfield, *Biblical Doctrines* (New York: Oxford University Press, 1929), 141–42.

4 Matthew 5:45; 6:1, 4, 6, 8, 9, 14, 15, 18 (twice), 32; 7:11, 21.

5 Paul uses this illustration in Galatians 3:22–4:7.

6 In the technical sense of *apologetic*, i.e., not apologizing in the sense of saying "sorry" but in the sense of speaking on behalf of or in defense of the Christian faith. It is in this sense that Peter uses the word *apologia* in 1 Peter 3:15.

7 In his *The Essence of Christianity*, Feuerbach uses the expression "theology is anthropology"—that is, when we talk about God, we are really talking about ourselves. His book was originally translated into English by Marian Evans (the real name of the novelist George Eliot): *The Essence of Christianity* (London: Kegan Paul, Trench, Trubner & Co., 1893), xi, 270, 301.

8 One of Schleiermacher's early works was *On Religion: Speeches to Its Cultured Despisers* (1799).

9 *The Works of John Owen*, ed. W.H. Goold (1850–53; repr., Edinburgh, Scotland: Banner of Truth Trust, 1965–68), 2:22–23.

10 *Works of John Owen*, 2:32.

Chapter 11

1 Leviticus 16:8 explains the drawing of lots over the two goats, "one lot for the LORD and the other lot for Azazel." Since "Azazel" was the name of a pagan demon, the significance of the second goat has been much debated by scholars. Perhaps the best way to understand the picture is to think of the first goat as a sacrifice symbolizing the need for the forgive-

ness of sins, while the second goat is taken out into the domain of the evil one.

Christ fulfills this dramatic representation. In His sacrifice of Himself, He makes atonement for the guilt of sin, but He also enters the domain of Satan, conquers him, and releases us from our bondage to him. God had made a twofold provision for sin in Eden: the covering of guilt and shame by means of the garments provided by a sacrifice and deliverance from the serpent, provided by the promise (Gen. 3:15, 21). The Day of Atonement made this even clearer. The day that was about to dawn would make it clearer still.

2 The ESV (2016) translates *pais* as "servant" and puts the translation "child" in a footnote. Elsewhere it translates *pais* as "boy" when used of Jesus in Luke 2:43. There is some theological value in translating *pais* as "child" in Acts 3 in order to bring out the fact that in relation to the heavenly Father, the eternal Son was *obedient* during the days of His flesh. This is the specific form of "honor" appropriate to the incarnation.

The fifth commandment as such implies that a son should *honor* his father. This is true for us whether we are children or adults. "Honor" takes the form of *obedience* so long as our condition (e.g., as minors) places us under the authority of our father. In adult life, a son is no longer under the authority of a father to obey him in the same way ("a man shall leave his father and his mother . . . ," Gen. 2:24). But he must always honor him. Since the commandments are a reflection of God Himself, by way of analogy we might say that the second person of the Trinity always honors the Father whose Son He is, but in sharing our humanity that "honor" takes the specific form of submissive obedience. Thus, as the eternal Son, He eternally *honors* His Father, but His eternal relationship with His Father is not one of eternal *subordination*.

3 Cf. Westminster Confession of Faith 2.3.

4 Other indications of our Lord's conscious sense that He shared the divine nature are present in John 17, for example in the way He describes the disciples as "in us" (v. 21).

5 Westminster Shorter Catechism 1.

6 *Oxford English Dictionary*, s.v. "hiareth, *n.*," accessed June 24, 2020, https://www.oed.com/view/Entry/85866024?redirectedFrom=hiraeth#eid.

7 After a remarkable career as surgeon-in-chief at the Children's Hospital of Philadelphia, Dr. C. Everett Koop (1916–2013) served as surgeon general of the United States from 1982 to 1989.

Chapter 12

1 From the hymn "Jesus, the Very Thought of Thee," sometimes attributed to Bernard of Clairvaux, and translated by Edward Caswall (1814–78).

2 From the hymn "A Mighty Fortress Is Our God" by Martin Luther, translated by Frederick H. Hedge.

Chapter 13

1 Lest there be a theological quibble here, on the basis that God is "one substance," we should note that the analogy Jesus draws is not between the unity of believers and the unity of God's being but between the nature of the fellowship of the members of the church and the fellowship between the distinct persons of the Father and the Son.

2 This would lead to the heresy known as Modalism—that the Father, Son, and Spirit are simply manifestations of the one and not three distinct persons sharing one and the same being.

3 This became an essential element in the formulation of the doctrine of the Trinity: the three persons of the Godhead share one being or substance and are distinguished only by their properties of paternity (the Father), filiation (the Son), and procession (the Spirit). Cf. Westminster Confession of Faith 2.3: "In the unity of the Godhead there be three persons, of one substance, power, and eternity; God the Father, God the Son, and God the Holy Ghost."

Index

Abba, 168, 171

Abel, 120

abiding in Christ, 106, 110–11, 113–14, 116–17, 179

Acts (book of), 48, 81–82, 107, 127, 154–55, 203, 213, 219

Adam, 120, 188–190

Advocate, 91–92, 98

alienation, 216

allegory, 191, 194

"A Mighty Fortress Is Our God," 232

Ananias, 127, 219

ancient Near East, 53

Ancient of Days, 48–50

Andrew, 76

angel of light, 126

angels, 34, 55, 123, 194

Annas, 4, 151

anthropomorphism, 168

apologetics, 168

Apostles, 8, 25, 27, 37, 59, 63, 69, 79–81, 89, 136, 140, 144, 153–55, 168, 182, 200, 202–4, 209, 212–13, 219–20

Apostolic ministry, 7, 27, 182, 204, 222

Aramaic, 53

archangels, 55, 194

ark of the covenant, 179–180

Asaph, 163

ascension (of Christ), 22, 50, 53, 55, 58, 103, 108, 149, 151, 160, 189, 213

Augustine (of Hippo), 57, 99

authority (of Christ), 12, 17–18, 44, 51, 62, 78, 104, 123, 137–38, 142, 177, 186, 188–90

authority (of Scripture), 204

Azazel, 180

Babylon, 120

baptism, 15, 93, 152

beast, 49–50, 125

Beatitudes, 33

Bethany, 39, 70

Bethesda, 151

Bethlehem, 15

betrayal (of Christ), 3–6, 11, 15–16, 26–28, 35–41, 43, 46, 64, 83, 121, 183

Bible study, 63, 114

blessed, 19, 21, 32–33, 71, 115, 186

blessings, 22, 127, 163

blood, 29, 31, 37, 51, 53, 58, 123, 131, 174, 180–181, 195

bondservants, 25, 29, 31–32, 144

Book of Glory, 8, 178
Book of Signs, 7, 121, 178
Book of the Passion, 8
Booths (Feast of), 182
branches, 105–6, 109–10, 112, 122, 166
Bread of Life, 77, 166
Bunyan, John, 135

Caiaphas, 4, 51, 151, 161
Cain, 120
calling, 25, 51, 54, 63, 128, 168, 189, 195
Calvary, 4, 15, 22, 54, 56, 212, 220, 222
Calvin, John, 8, 46
Cana, 182, 185
Carmichael, Amy, 112
Cash, Pat, 221
catechism, 187
chain of glory, 202
Charles Wesley, 13
cherubim, 194
Christ, 1–3, 5–9, 11, 13–19, 23, 26–30, 32–34, 36–37, 41–43, 46, 50–51, 53–56, 58–59, 65–69, 72–73, 80, 82–83, 91, 94, 98, 100–103, 106–16, 120–23, 125, 127, 129, 131–36, 139–40, 143–44, 147, 151–52, 154–56, 164–65, 167, 172–74, 176–79, 181, 183, 185–91, 193, 195–96, 201, 203–5, 213–15, 217–18, 220–21
Christ of St. John of the Cross, 36
church, 28, 54, 59, 69, 79, 82, 95, 98, 103, 111, 125–30, 134–35, 139–40, 143, 153, 168, 182, 202, 209, 213–16, 218–20
church family, 111, 125, 214–16, 218
Chytraeus, David, 212
cleansing (from sin), 10, 14–15, 117, 143
Colossians, 214
communion, 55, 174, 189
Counselor (Holy Spirit), 91, 93–94, 146
Cowper, William, 162–63
creation, 18, 50, 109, 127, 170, 188, 190, 216
Creator, 66, 166
cross (of Calvary), 4, 10–11, 14–16, 36–37, 42, 46, 48, 52–55, 72, 74–75, 128–29, 147, 152, 164, 182–83, 191, 222
crucifixion, 4, 48, 52–53, 64, 74, 194, 212

Dalí, Salvador 36–37
Daniel, 48, 50–51
dark, 15, 36–37, 43, 46–47, 54, 104, 138, 163, 173
David, 50, 120, 212
Day of Atonement, 179–181, 199, 212
death, 8, 10–11, 15–16, 18, 29, 33, 47–48, 50, 52–54, 58, 64, 75, 121, 124, 131, 151, 160–61, 182–83, 188–89, 192
devil, 3, 5, 11, 15, 44, 104, 120, 123–127, 131, 183, 208
discernment, 40, 144–145, 147, 159

disciples, 1, 3, 5–6, 8–11, 13,
15–18, 22–24, 26–27, 29,
33–35, 38–39, 43, 45–46, 48,
54, 56–57, 63–71, 78, 81–83,
87–88, 90–96, 98–100, 102–
110, 113, 117, 121–122, 126,
128–130, 133–134, 136–139,
142–143, 145, 147–150, 152,
155–166, 168, 171, 174–176,
178–181, 195, 198–202,
204–205, 207–208, 214–215,
217, 221
discipleship, 122, 162

Easter, 153, 161, 190
Eden, garden of, 50, 125, 50,
188–90
Egypt, 72, 109, 150
election, 200
Elisha, 130
Emmaus, 103, 160, 165
England, 124, 221
eternal life, 131, 172, 177, 186,
188–89
European Enlightenment, 169
evangelism, 215–216, 219
evil, 28, 40, 44, 104, 148, 181, 198
Ezekiel, 10, 48

faith, 6, 15, 26, 65–69, 73, 76, 80,
82, 108, 117, 129, 131–32, 137,
148, 168–69, 172–73, 196, 201,
215, 220
Father, 3, 5, 11–12, 15–18, 22, 27,
44, 47, 51–54, 56–57, 61–62,
67–68, 71–79, 83, 85–87,

89–91, 93, 95–100, 102, 104–8,
110–12, 116–17, 119–22,
130–34, 136–42, 146, 149,
151, 157–60, 163–78, 181–90,
194–97, 199–209, 211–14,
217–18, 220–23
fellowship, 58, 77, 99, 103, 111,
115, 117, 134, 173, 206,
213–18
foot-washing, 10, 14, 22–23,
26–28, 51, 143, 198
forgiveness, 42, 54, 73, 108, 152
Freud, Sigmund, 169
fruit (spiritual), 26, 101, 105–7,
110–12, 115–17, 127–29,
132–33
fruitfulness, 110–11, 116, 127
fruit of the Spirit, 112, 117, 133

George (saint), 124
Gethsemane, garden of, 4, 22, 38,
54, 56, 83, 104, 180, 212, 220
gifts (spiritual), 79, 101, 208
glorification, 47–48, 52–53
glory, 8, 10, 12, 18, 22, 26, 34, 44,
47–49, 51, 53–56, 58, 69, 72,
99, 101, 108, 110–11, 114, 133,
156, 162–66, 177, 183–89, 191,
195, 199, 202, 204–5, 211–12,
217–18, 220–23
Golden Rule, 24
Goliath, 120
Goodwin, Thomas, 1
gospel, 10, 23–24, 31, 41, 43, 52,
57, 64, 67, 100–101, 121–22,
127–29, 131, 133, 135, 137, 144,

150, 161, 171–72, 176, 178,
188, 190, 206, 214, 216, 222
Gospels, 8, 15, 38, 40, 76, 92,
154–155, 185, 198, 203
grace, 7, 14, 18, 22, 25–26, 32–34,
41–43, 47, 72–73, 101, 117,
131, 133, 143, 148, 167, 215
guilt, 24, 41–42, 64, 128, 150,
180–81

Hades, 213
happiness, 33, 98, 186
heaven, 10, 18, 26, 49, 51, 55,
67–69, 72, 74–75, 79, 95, 123,
131, 133, 139, 149–50, 166,
177, 183, 188, 194–95, 208–9
Hebrews, 43, 191
Heidelberg Catechism, 29, 131
Helper, 85–91, 98, 102, 104, 120,
122, 135–36, 139, 141, 146,
149, 202
Herod, 4, 15, 120, 151
high priest, 4, 179–80, 195, 199,
206, 212
High Priest (Jesus), 181, 190
holiness, 52, 102, 115, 191, 194,
219
Holy of Holies, 176, 179
Holy Place, 179
Holy Spirit, 25, 38, 40, 43, 47,
52–53, 63, 81, 85–89, 91–103,
106, 108, 110–12, 117, 120,
122, 126, 131, 133, 136–38,
140, 142–43, 145, 148–56,
168, 174–76, 178, 191, 194,
200–205, 208, 213–15, 218, 223

homesickness, 38, 191, 195
humiliation, 12–13, 17, 50, 83,
110
humility, 13–14, 25–27, 32, 46

image of Christ, 114, 164
incarnation, 13, 50, 161, 185, 218
individualism, 216
indwelling of the Spirit, 91, 98,
100–103, 106, 108, 111, 139,
156, 214, 218
intercession, 91, 180, 182,
199–200, 209, 213
Isaiah, 7, 17, 50, 148
Israel, 166, 179–180, 212

Jerusalem, 4, 8, 70, 81, 104, 109,
120, 127, 150, 152, 160, 179,
188, 219
Jesus, 1–18, 22–36, 38–48, 50–59,
61–74, 76–83, 85, 87–104,
106–10, 112–17, 121–22,
124–40, 142–68, 170–84,
186–91, 194, 196, 198–208,
212–15, 217–22
as Example, 22, 26
as Savior, 22, 26
Farewell Discourse of, 2
High Priestly Prayer of, 182,
187–88, 190–91, 202,
212, 215–19
as Lamb of God, 59, 72–73,
123
as last Adam, 189
as Light of the World, 7, 72,
166

ministry of, 10, 14, 39, 47, 50, 76, 82, 87–88, 90–94, 98–100, 103, 121, 139–40, 145, 148, 166, 181–82, 189, 199, 209
passion of, 52
prayer of, 5, 115, 178–80, 182–84, 187–88, 190–91, 196, 198–99, 201–3, 205, 212–20, 223
second coming of, 51, 67–68, 82, 121
as servant, 10, 13, 17, 22, 25, 50–51, 58, 182
Son of God, 13–14, 31, 43, 48, 52, 65, 74, 91, 102, 111, 166, 171, 184, 191, 205, 209
Son of Man, 36, 45, 46–48, 50–52, 134
Suffering Servant, 17, 50–51
Sun of Righteousness, 133
union with, 15, 100, 107–8, 110–16, 125, 166
as the Word, 12–13, 26, 29, 37, 40, 47, 71, 72, 77–78, 99, 139, 145, 166, 188
Jews, 45, 150, 214
John (Apostle), 2, 5, 8, 11–12, 15–17, 22–23, 26–27, 33, 36–38, 40, 47, 54–56, 58, 63, 71–73, 76–78, 87, 91, 94, 98–99, 104, 121–122, 124–125, 142, 144, 150–151, 160, 166, 172, 178–179, 185, 190, 212, 217
Jonah, 59

joy, 46, 51, 55, 69, 106, 117, 145, 156–58, 161–65, 172, 175, 187, 191, 198, 208, 223
Judas Iscariot, 3, 5, 11, 15–16, 26–27, 31, 35–36, 38–44, 46–47, 85, 96, 121, 142, 145, 151, 178, 198, 206
judgment, 38, 49, 75, 121, 132–34, 141–42, 149, 152, 190, 220
justification, 14

Kant, Immanuel, 169
King James Version, 180
kingdom of God, 49–51, 82, 123, 129–30, 146, 153, 159, 192, 208, 216
kingdom of heaven, 79
Koop, C. Everett, 196

Latin, 53, 73, 229
Lazarus, 47–48, 70, 151
Lewis, C.S., 97, 139
light, 36, 56, 94, 104, 114, 126, 133–34, 160, 167, 173, 175
Ligonier Ministries, 1–2
living water, 166
living Word, 72
Lord of glory, 22, 26, 34, 108, 111
Lordship (of Christ), 14
love, 2, 5, 7, 9, 13, 24, 26–27, 33, 41, 45, 53–58, 67, 74, 82, 85–86, 90, 92, 94, 96, 100, 102, 104–6, 116–17, 119, 126, 143–44, 147, 156, 171–75, 178, 189, 194, 196, 199–202, 209, 211, 214, 220, 222–23

Luke (evangelist), 9, 82
Luke, gospel of, 8
Luther, Martin, 44, 66, 86, 207, 232

majesty, 12, 58, 132, 185
martyr, 134
Marx, Karl, 169–170
Mary (mother of Jesus), 93, 108, 137
Mary Magdalene, 171, 190
Mary of Bethany, 39, 41
Melanchthon, Philip, 66
mercy, 39, 68, 127, 163
mercy seat, 180
Messiah, 7, 66, 71, 151
military, 104, 121
ministry of the Spirit, 92, 94, 96,
    98, 102–3, 155, 176, 204
ministry of the Word, 115, 145
miracles, 39, 79–80
Mosaic law, 73
Moses, 50, 71–72, 92, 120, 167
Most Holy Place, 179
Mount of Transfiguration, 185, 194

Nazareth, 4–5, 47, 53
new commandment, 45, 56–57
new covenant, 101, 126, 181
new creation, 109, 127, 216
new identity, 108, 111, 128
new Jerusalem, 188
New Testament, 5, 31, 33, 43, 48,
    53, 90–91, 101, 103, 107, 114,
    120, 139–40, 154–56, 162,
    166–67, 178, 181–82, 185, 201,
    203–6, 213, 216
Nicene Creed, 98

obedience, 90, 115, 116–17, 189
obedience of Christ, 51–52, 116,
    184
old covenant, 71–73, 101, 168,
    179, 181
Old Testament, 17, 22, 50, 72–73,
    120, 166–68, 184

pagans, 57
Paraclete, 98, 100, 102–103
paraklētos, 89–93, 136–137
Passover, 3–5, 8–9, 11, 39
Patmos, 122, 185
Paul (Apostle), 10–11, 13, 24, 29,
    31, 65, 73, 79, 91, 99–101, 107,
    110–11, 114–115, 133, 144,
    151, 154, 161, 175, 181, 183,
    187, 214, 217, 221
peace, 64, 86, 132, 158, 174, 176
Pentecost, 53, 99, 136, 138,
    150–53, 215
persecution, 127–28, 133, 138, 146
Peter (Apostle). See Simon Peter
Philip, 61, 70, 76–78, 178
Pilate, Pontius, 4, 52–53, 151
plan of salvation, 15
power (of God), 8, 12, 15, 24, 39,
    52–53, 67–68, 77, 93, 123, 130,
    135, 184–85, 219
powers of darkness, 51, 121
prayer, 82, 113, 117, 205, 223
prophecy, 27, 40, 59, 81–82, 136,
    150, 154
prophet, 7, 71, 73, 156
Protestant Reformation, 86
Psalms, 71, 183

purification, 72, 206
Puritan, 1, 107

Redeemer, 8
Reformation, 66, 86, 179
Rembrandt, 36
restoration, 50, 153, 176, 187,
    189–90
resurrection, 8, 17, 48, 50, 52–53,
    58, 68, 130, 137, 151, 160–61,
    165, 171, 189–90, 213
Revelation, book of, 33, 154–155,
    203
righteousness, 53, 101, 141–142,
    149, 151–152
Roman Empire, 25, 53

sacrament, 28
sacrifice, 31, 179–81, 201
sacrifices, 73, 82, 179, 181, 212
salvation, 6, 14–15, 22–23, 44, 54,
    68–69, 123, 131, 200, 216
sanctification, 15, 117, 198,
    204–207, 212, 219
Sapphira, 127
Satan, 15–16, 27, 35, 104,
    120–121, 123–125, 127, 129,
    134, 218
Saul of Tarsus, 127, 139
Savior, 5, 7, 18, 22–24, 26, 29,
    38–40, 42–43, 47–48, 53–54,
    58–59, 66, 94, 128, 131, 139,
    149, 152, 155, 171, 176, 182,
    191, 209, 213
Schaeffer, Francis, 37
Schleiermacher, Friedrich, 169

Scotland, 120, 187
Scottish Presbyterians, 55
Sea of Galilee, 65, 76, 82, 206
seed of the serpent, 16, 121
Seed of the woman, 16, 50,
    121–22, 124, 128
Sermon on the Mount, 33, 79, 167
serpent, 16, 40, 44, 72, 120–25,
    127, 183, 190
servant of Jesus, 18–19, 25, 28–29,
    32, 34, 106, 119, 129
service, 14, 18, 30–31, 62, 69, 95,
    112, 141, 181, 185
seventeenth century, 107
Simon Peter, 3–7, 9, 14–16,
    22–23, 25–26, 31, 35, 38, 45,
    57–59, 68–70, 73–74, 107, 113,
    136–37, 142, 148, 150–51, 153,
    156, 178, 194, 198, 201, 205–6,
    216, 223
sin offering, 180
slave, 10, 25, 30, 34, 43, 214
sovereign, 27, 44, 163
Spirit-breathed, 204
spiritual bondage, 181
spiritual vitality, 213
Stephen, 48, 127, 134, 136, 139
suffering, 17, 37, 74, 83, 112, 128,
    133, 145, 162–64
Synoptic Gospels, 8, 185

tabernacle, 179, 188
temple, 43, 104, 179, 185
temptation, 134
temptations of Christ, 93
Ten Commandments, 116

Tertullian, 57
Thessalonians, 115
Thomas, 61, 70–73, 76, 178
tribulation, 158, 162, 164, 176, 179
Trinity (doctrine of the), 99, 138–
    39, 143, 145, 195, 200–201
understanding, 8, 23–24, 34, 91, 99,
    103, 112, 143–45, 155–56, 159
United States, 187, 196
unity of believers, 213–15, 217–18
upper room, 2, 4–5, 24–26, 33,
    36–37, 46–47, 56, 63, 70, 91,
    98, 104, 109, 121, 125, 127,
    129, 139–40, 142, 153, 155,
    159, 170–71, 175, 182, 204–5,
    209, 212, 220

Van Gogh, Vincent, 36
Via Dolorosa, 4, 51, 212

vine, 105–7, 109–13, 115, 117,
    122, 166
vinedresser, 105–6, 110, 112–13
Virgin Mary, 93
Vulgate, 73

wages of sin, 53, 64
Warfield, B.B., 167
Whitehead, Alfred North, 120
will of God, 16–17, 29, 79, 82,
    113, 131, 174, 213, 221, 223
witness for Christ, 120, 129,
    134, 136–40, 146, 155, 215,
    221–22
Word of God, 29, 40, 43, 113–17,
    145, 155–56, 202, 205, 207–8,
    219, 223

Yahweh, 184

About the Author

Dr. Sinclair B. Ferguson is a Ligonier teaching fellow and Chancellor's Professor of Systematic Theology at Reformed Theological Seminary. He previously served as senior minister of the historic First Presbyterian Church in Columbia, S.C.

Dr. Ferguson is a native of Scotland and earned his Ph.D. at the University of Aberdeen. He was a minister of two churches in Scotland, on the island of Unst, the most northerly of the Shetland Islands, and in St. George's-Tron (now known as the Tron Church), in the city center of Glasgow. He has authored many books, including *Devoted to God, The Whole Christ, The Holy Spirit, In Christ Alone, The Sermon on the Mount,* and *Devoted to God's Church.*